Contents

About the contributors

Irina Anderson, Department of Psychology, University of Sheffield

Geoffrey Beattie, Department of Psychology, University of Sheffield

Graham Beck, HMYOI Lancaster Farms

Ronald Blackburn, Departments of Psychology and Psychiatry, University of Liverpool and Research Unit, Ashworth Hospital

Mary Boyle, Department of Psychology, University of East London

Ray Bull, Department of Psychology, University of Portsmouth

Anne Carpenter, Douglas Insch Centre

John B. Copas, Department of Statistics, University of Warwick

Polly M. Dexter, HMP Highpoint

William Fulford, Research Fellow in Philosophy at Green College, Oxford and Honorary Consultant Psychiatrist at the Warneford Hospital

Patricia Hind, Department of Psychology, City University

Gunter Koehnken, Department of Psychology, University of Portsmouth

Helen Liebling, Ashworth Hospital

Juliana MacLeod, Dr Gray's Hospital, Elgin

Mick McKeown, Ashworth Hospital

Amina Memon, Department of Psychology, University of Southampton

Rebecca Milne, Department of Psychology, University of Portsmouth

Sarah Skett, HMYOI and RC Glen Parva

Helen L. Westcott, Research Office, NSPCC National Centre, London

Graham J. Towl, HMP Highpoint

Gender differences in attributional reasoning about rape during actual conversation

Irina Anderson and Geoffrey Beattie

A central psychological concept in criminological and legal psychology is the concept of the attribution – how people reason about the causality of any particular act or criminal event. In the case of rape, the attributions made are particularly significant, indeed these are considered to be one of the major factors in the low rate of successful prosecution for rape. There has been a great deal of psychological research into the kinds of factors that affect attributional reasoning about rape, including victim characteristics, pre-attack behaviours, victim resistance, victim-attacker acquaintance and many others. The problem with the research reviewed by Pollard is that subjects are invariably constrained to questionnaires on which they are asked to make a variety of judgements with regard to the assignment of responsibility and blame to the victim and attacker. The present study is one of the first to attempt to analyse attributions in spontaneous conversation, in an attempt to use a much more naturalistic form of approach to the issues.

Introduction

This study looks at how people attribute responsibility for cases of rape. We argue that this is an important area of research because such attributions will affect whether victims, taking advice from those around them, will ever report the crime. We thus see ourselves as investigating one aspect of psychological functioning which affects the under reporting of crime in general.

Recent Home Office statistics reveal that the reporting of rape is on the increase, with 4,100 rape offences recorded in 1992, an increase of two per cent from 1991 and over three times the number recorded in 1980. Much of this recent increase is thought to be attributable both to an increase in reporting by the public, and to changes in police practice, resulting in an increasing proportion of reported cases actually being recorded as offences. However, rape continues to have the lowest clear-up rate of any crime apart from abduction and, despite changing public attitudes, remains grossly under reported, with estimates varying from anything between 50 and 90 per cent of cases going unreported. One reason for this may be the result of the way people with whom the rape victim comes into contact, in both the short-term and the long-term, such as the rape victims' family and friends, doctors, nurses and the police, attribute responsibility for the act.

A large number of studies have tried to determine the kinds of factors which affect attributions of responsibility in rape. The majority of such studies have relied on a relatively standard method for investigating these factors and their effect on subsequent attributions. Subjects, usually North American undergraduates, are given a brief written scenario of a rape (the vignette) and are asked to make a variety of judgements, usually to assign responsibility, fault or blame to the victim and the attacker, and sometimes to recommend a prison sentence. Invariably, these studies have used paper-and-pencil tasks where subjects are asked to make judgements using a questionnaire. With this technique, studies have identified a whole range of factors which affect attributions of responsibility in rape (see Pollard, 1992). For example, it has been found that victim characteristics such as respectability (Luginbuhl and Mullin, 1981), physical attractiveness (Deitz et al., 1984), previous sexual experience (L'Armand and Pepitone, 1982), and history of rape (Calhoun et al., 1976), all affect victim perception. Other factors which have been identified include: victim attacker acquaintance (Bridges and McGrail, 1989); the degree to which the victim resisted the assault (Scroggs, 1976); victim's pre-attack behaviour such as the degree of intoxication (Richardson and Campbell, 1982); whether she took any precautions (Pallack and Davies, 1982); whether she was "sexily" dressed (Edmonds and Cahoon, 1986); and the area in which the victim found herself (Calhoun et al., 1976).

All these factors have been found to affect the strength of attributions of blame, fault and responsibility, made to the rape victim. In addition, a very consistent finding is that male subjects make stronger attributions of blame, fault and responsibility to the victim than female subjects. However, what many of these studies lack is a theoretical model of the kinds of attributional processing which may operate when males and females are asked to consider a rape scenario. The study by Calhoun et al. (1976) into the social perception of the rape victim's causal role in rape is an interesting exception which, in addition, highlights some potential gender differences in the reasoning males and females may employ when making attributions about the causal factors involved in rape. Calhoun et al.'s study is based upon one particular model of the attribution process - Kelley's Co-variation Model (1967). Attribution theory in general is concerned with how people explain causality of events and the most widely researched model which delineates this process is the co-variation model. The basic premise of this model is that any behaviour or event can be considered in terms of "actor", "behaviour" and "stimulus", and the cause of any such target event can be attributed to one of the involved entities. For example, to take a well-known stimulus sentence from a traditional attributional study (McArthur, 1972), "John laughs at the comedian", John, in this case is the actor, "laughs" is the behaviour and the comedian is the stimulus. To decide which factor is the cause, the observer will need to consider information about how other people behave towards the stimulus (consensus), whether the actor has behaved in the same way towards the stimulus on other occasions (consistency), and whether the actor behaves in the same way to other stimuli (distinctiveness). In addition, these information variables can be coded to indicate whether the target event occurs in the presence or absence of each of the possible causes. In the case of John, if other people also laugh at the comedian (high consensus), if John has laughed at this comedian in the past (high consistency), and if John does not laugh at any other comedian (high distinctiveness, where the behaviour is distinctive to this particular stimulus), the logical attribution is to the comedian, or the stimulus. Differently coded configurations of the variables of consensus, distinctiveness and consistency will produce other attributions, namely to the actor or to the circumstances.

Although it may at first sight seem difficult to conceptualize a rape in terms of the "John laughs at the comedian" type of script, this is nevertheless quite possible when we encode it as "rapist (actor) rapes (behaviour) victim (stimulus)". Furthermore, Calhoun et al.'s study does provide evidence that subjects may be using the dimensions of consensus, distinctiveness and consistency when considering a rape vignette. Specifically, Calhoun et al.'s questionnaire study showed that males were attributing highest blame to the victim specifically under the configuration of high consensus/consistency and high distinctiveness - in other words, when the information specified that the victim had been raped before (presumably different rapists, therefore high consistency and high consensus) and there had been no other rapes in the area (high distinctiveness). This is, of course, precisely the configuration of dimensions which Kelley's model predicts to lead the observer to a stimulus attribution. Females, however, made the strongest attributions of blame to the victim when she had been raped before (high consistency/high consensus), but when there had also been other rapes in the area (low distinctiveness). This configuration of variables deviates from any of Kelley's attributional predictions. Calhoun et al.'s interpretation of these results suggested that males follow the kind of logic advocated by Kelley's model, the logic deriving from traditional attribution theory.

Females, on the other hand, Calhoun argued, appeared to adopt the interpretation that the victim "should have known better" than to be in an environment where rapes had occurred, in other words, the victim should have foreseen the possibility that she could be raped again. This, however, was offered simply as a post-hoc interpretation of the results. The purpose of the research reported here was to test this possible interpretation of the gender difference, but to test it in a very different domain from previous questionnaire-based research. The point has already been made that the majority of rape studies have constrained subjects to paper-and-pencil tasks. A similar criticism has been levelled at research on Kelley's attribution model generally suggesting that:

Its operational convenience quickly shackled attribution theory to a punishingly tight paradigm ... It was impossible to do empirical work on Kelley's model in anything other than paper-and-pencil form. If you allowed subjects to simply explain in normal conversation then you faced the virtually impossible task of classifying what they said into the model's tripartite causal system. But since there seems to be no published accounts in social psychology journals of anyone actually having struggled to fit the Kelley model to talk, the issue has simply disappeared. (Antaki and Leudar, 1992)

The purpose of our series of studies was to test whether Calhoun et al.'s gender differences would emerge in an attributional task involving a rape when subjects were asked to talk about, rather than answer questions on, a rape scenario and whether these differences would specifically arise from differences in the implementation of Kelley's model.

Study 1. Kelley variables and foreseeability in conversation

The purpose of this study was to see whether Kelley's variables of consensus, distinctiveness and consistency, and the variable of foreseeability actually occurred in conversation. The particular configuration of Kelley's variables used here were that the victim had been raped before (high consensus/consistency) and that there had been other rapes in the area (low distinctiveness), which is the combination which Calhoun et al. argued led to attributions using the construct of foreseeability as favoured by the female subjects. It should be noted that this particular combination, in principle, does allow a variety of types of attributions (following Kelley). The high consensus/high consistency manipulation should lead logically to a stimulus attribution (something about the victim). The low distinctiveness manipulation should lead to an attribution to the actor (something about the rapist).

Method

Four male/male, four male/female and four female/female pairs of subjects (all university students) were presented with a vignette (with the Kelley variables embedded) and were asked to discuss the incident of the alleged rape, which is replicated below. They were also asked to reach a conclusion.

A 22-year-old single woman testified in court that she was raped in the campus of a middle-sized university where she was attending as a full-time student. On the evening of the attack, the woman had taken a short-cut home through the badly lit campus after attending a dance class. The alleged rape took place at 9.30pm, when the woman was attacked and dragged away from the main path and sexually assaulted. The woman told the court that she was aware of a man walking behind her, but this had not aroused any suspicion in her. The woman's screams from the attack were heard and a passer-by arrived and chased the attacker away. This passer-by subsequently identified the accused in a police line-up. The woman had been raped once before about one year prior to this attack. It was known that five other women had been sexually assaulted on the campus in the past six months before this alleged rape took place.

Will the Kelley variables and the variable of foreseeability (for example, the victim should have taken precautions, the victim should have been more careful, should have been more aware, etc.) occur in conversation? It was found that both males and females referred to both concepts but males referred to Kelley's variables significantly more frequently than females ($U=7$, $n1=8$, $n2=8$, $p.01$) while females referred to foreseeability significantly more frequently than males ($U=18$, $n1=12$, $n2=12$, $p.01$). (See Table 1a.)

In addition, were the Kelley variables and the variable of foreseeability being used to attribute causality to the victim as other rape studies and Kelley's model would suggest? A rather mechanical, but nevertheless previously used method (for example, see Antaki and Naji, 1987), was to look for instances of Kelley variables and the variable of foreseeability together with the causal connective "because". It was found that, although such utterances occurred relatively infrequently in the conversational corpus, males nevertheless made attributions to the victim together with the causal connective "because" more often than females, who almost never did this (only one instance actually recorded). Females, on the other hand, referred to the variable of foreseeability together with the causal connective "because" slightly more frequently than males.

Table 1a shows the mean frequency of occurrence of each concept, and Table 1b shows the total frequencies of occurrence of Kelley variables and the concept of foreseeability, together with the causal connective "because". The following are some examples of such utterances:

Kelley variables
M: for a start she has been raped before.
M: yeah and there had been other rapes in the area.

Foreseeability variables
F: there appears to have been no foreseeability on her part at all that she might be in danger.
M: she shouldn't have walked down there should she because + Kelley M: she was rather stupid though 'cos there've been other rapes reported.
F: but what is she supposed to do never go out because + foreseeability F: no but that's absolutely ridiculous if people carry on thinking like that then nothing will be done about rapes. Okay she was stupid cos she didn't avoid an area that was bad but it shouldn't happen in the first place should it.
M: yeah I suppose so.

Table 1a. Mean frequency of occurrence of Kelley variables and variable of foreseeability per subject

	Kelley	Foreseeability
male subjects	4.88**	3.41
female subjects	1.98	5.50**

** p 0.01 (Mann-Whitney U test)

Table 1b. Total frequency of occurrence of Kelley variables and variable of foreseeability together with causal connective "because"

	because + Kelley	because + Foreseeability
male subjects	8	6
female subjects	1	11

It would appear that there is some evidence to suggest that males indeed utilize Kelley's variables when attributing the cause of the rape to the victim, whereas females diverge from Kelley's logic to attribute causality to the victim in terms of foreseeability, i.e. that "she should have taken precautions", "been more aware" and "been more careful".

Study 2. Negative attributions to rape victims in conversation

This study was specifically concerned with whether males and females actually make negative attributions to the rape victim and whether they specifically refer to fault and blame in discussing rape. In this study, the data was provided by six male/female pairs (again university students), who were asked to talk about the same scenario as that of Study 1. The analysis revealed that male subjects specifically stated that they blamed the victim and that it was her fault (including that she was "asking for it") three times as often as female subjects. They made negative attributions specifically to characteristics of the victim more than twice as often as the female subjects. For example (/ indicates a short pause in talk; // indicates a long pause):

Blame, fault and "asking for it"
M: mm // I blame her / I think she asked for it

Negative attributions to characteristics of victim
M: she's pretty stupid seeings as / what is it / five other people had been assaulted there / I mean 9.30pm it's going to be dark

To summarize, it would appear that men draw upon Kelley's variables to make attributions regarding the victim's causal role in rape. Females, however, seem to diverge from Kelley's model by evoking the concept of foreseeability. In addition, consistent with previous findings, males make more negative attributions to the rape victim than females. What accounts for these gender differences? Males' and females' talk was examined for any differences in the kinds of themes contained in them. The following are some of the issues which came up and which may help to explain the gender differences observed.

Reasoning experience
F: I was thinking about this the other day.

Motivation to consider rape
M: yeah we were saying that when we watched *The Accused* it got us thinking that they were insinuating it was the clothes that she wore that got her raped.

Likelihood of rape
F: and they say that rape/the incidence of rape is increasing all the time so women are more in danger than before.

Reality of this rape case
M: this is only a hypothetical case.

Empathy
F: yeah I walked back from aerobics on my own yesterday / you could imagine the same thing happening.

Emotion
F: it really makes me angry things like this.

The concepts contained in the above utterances may be grouped under two broad dimensions - a cognitive dimension (knowledge about rape, thinking and reasoning experience) and an emotional dimension (anger, empathy, etc.). One reason for the observed gender differences may be that because of the very real threat that the issue of rape has for females not only is identification with a rape victim particularly strong, but the practical consequences of reasoning, thinking and talking about rape are of far greater importance for females than for males.

It has previously been proposed (Shaver's Defensive Attribution Hypothesis, 1970) that because males cannot imagine themselves in the role of a rape victim (although this may be changing with the recent increases in the reporting of cases of male rape), they have less strong identification with a victim of rape (who, up until recently, was generally thought to be female). Presumably, males would have less practical need to have thought, reasoned and talked about issues related to victimization in rape. One interpretation of the observed gender differences in Studies 1 and 2 is that when males are faced with discussing an issue that they have little previous reasoning experience about, they have to rely on Kelley's logic as a "default" position. In other words, it might be proposed that we use Kelley's dimensions to provide us with a framework for reasoning when we have little else to fall back on.

Alternatively, of course, you could argue that Kelley's model is the "logical" model for attributing causality in the world and that in the case of our female subjects, the emotional dimension somehow interferes with this. These different interpretations do require further investigation. In the meantime, we decided to test the generality of the gender difference in attributing causality in rape by changing the gender of the victim of rape. Will the male subject have a closer identification with the male rape victim, and if so, will the Kelley model become less salient? Will we see a reversal in that the female subjects may now rely on Kelley's variables to attribute causality in the case of male rape? This last study examined Kelley's model in a larger sample of male/female pairs discussing both female and male rape.

Study 3. Female and male rape in conversation

Method

Fifteen male/female pairs discussed female rape and eight male/female pairs discussed male rape (again, all university students). The configuration of Kelley variables embedded into the vignettes was the same as in the previous studies (raped before, other rapes in the area). Below is the vignette used in the male rape scenario:

A 22-year-old man testified that he was raped while travelling on an empty front carriage on the London Underground. He was on his way home from a meeting. The alleged rape took place at 9.30pm when a man clubbed him down and then sexually assaulted him. The victim said that he was aware the attacker was staring at him but this had not aroused his suspicion. The man had been raped once before around two years prior to the attack. Five other sexual attacks in the area, on men, had been well reported in local newspapers in the six months before this alleged rape had taken place.

Kelley variables

Table 2a illustrates the mean frequency of occurrence of the Kelley dimensions and Table 2b illustrates the total frequency of the occurrence of the causal connective "because" together with a Kelley variable for males and females when talking about female and male rape.

In female rape, consistent with previous findings, males mention Kelley variables significantly more frequently than females (t=2.19, df=14, p.05).

In male rape, there was no significant difference in the frequency of references to Kelley variables between males and females. Kelley variables together with the causal connective "because", occurred very infrequently in discussions of both female and male rape, but whereas such utterances were found more frequently in male than female speech in the case of female rape, the same pattern was not observed in the case of male rape.

Table 2a. Mean frequency of occurrence of Kelley dimensions in discussions of female and male rape

Kelley dimensions	female rape	male rape
male subjects	4.4*	2.6
female subjects	2.8	2.1

* p.05 (paired-scores *t* test)

Table 2b. Total frequency of occurrence of causal connective "because" with a Kelley dimension in female and male rape

"because" + Kelley dimension	female rape	male rape
male subjects	4	1
female subjects	1	2

Function of Kelley variables

The previous analysis concentrated solely on frequency of mentions of Kelley variables in male and female accounts of both rape scenarios. This section focuses on the actual function of Kelley variables and possible differences in their use by males and females. Some interesting differences in the use of the information that the victim had been raped before and that there had been some other rapes in the area were observed, where the variables were used specifically to make a number of attributions, namely to the victim, to any authority who could potentially be held responsible for the rape (in this case, the university campus through which the victim was walking and which was poorly lit), and to the authority and the victim both. In addition, some other, previously undocumented uses of Kelley's variables were observed, particularly in the females' speech, where the Kelley variable was used to mitigate responsibility to the victim by either undermining its logical implications or by challenging the usefulness of the Kelleyan information.

A separate category of "complex undermining" involved instances of the Kelley variable which were, on the one hand, presented as information which implied a negative attribution to the victim, but which later on in the conversational turn, were undermined. A residual category of "other" uses included comments on Kelley variables without any apparent attributional work being done (although these

Table 3. Functions of Kelley variables in female rape

	male subjects	female subjects
attribution to victim	34*	9
attribution to authority responsible for situation	4	5
attribution to victim and authority	6	0
undermine and challenge	2	12*
complex undermining	4	5
other	3	3

* p.05 (Wilcoxon Matched-Pairs Signed-Ranks Test)

may, of course, be also doing attributional work of some kind within the wider sequential structure of the conversation). Table 3 shows the function of these variables for female rape.

The following are some examples of the way in which males and females use Kelley's variables when discussing female rape.

Attribution to the victim
M: yeah yeah very naive in her attitude to say it's already happened once.
(F: oh yeah) she had a terrible experience before / it is strange it's not what you would expect.

Attribution to authority responsible for situation
F: ... if we were apportioning blame then / as we said right at the beginning of the discussion the blame surely lies with the university authorities and if I mean one rape is bad enough but there've been five or six I suppose counting this.

Attribution to victim and authority
M: she obviously wasn't being very careful, I mean fair enough, I mean nobody nobody's saying that she asked to be raped I am not saying that but it does say that she's been raped before / there was there've been other attacks on the campus I mean the university has got to hold some responsibility as to why it's a badly lit campus I mean that's just ludicrous.

Complex undermining
M: yeah but you would have thought the trauma of the first experience would have been enough to make her aware of the dangers / possible danger of it occurring again / and I suppose she I don't know / it's a terribly blase thing to say but she probably thought that lightning doesn't strike twice /I mean you're right well / I don't suppose she expects ever to you know a terrible thing like that can ever occur again.

Other
M: been raped once before

Undermining Kelley variables
F: so therefore she doesn't necessarily know that people that er women have been raped / in this area.
F: and as we all know this is horrible it won't happen to me / you know way of thinking and if / if it were that she'd been raped in a say a domestic scenario like in a claustrophobic way (M: mm) you know before / and then / she might not have connected the two like you say if she's had the experience of being raped in a totally different way (M: mm) then she'll probably associate this sort of scenario with even less / as somebody who'd been raped.
F: I think she thought well it's happened to me once it won't happen again.

Challenging Kelley variable
F: why does it say what has it got to do with it that she's already been raped.

There was a very striking difference in the use of the Kelley variables by males and females when discussing the female rape scenario. Males made attributions to the victim (these were all in fact negative attributions) to the victim significantly more frequently than females (T=10, df=12, p.02). Females, however, actively undermined the logic of the Kelley variables and challenged the usefulness of the information carried by the Kelley variables significantly more frequently than males (T=6, df=10, p.05).

Function of Kelley variables in male rape

Below are some examples of the way in which Kelley's variables were used in discussions of the male rape scenario.

Attribution to victim
M: I don't think he's very bright either if he's already been raped once
F: it says he's been raped once before though well maybe he's a bit of a wimp or something maybe he looked like an easy target

Undermining Kelley variable
F: yeah 'cos when it says erm five other sexual attacks in the area on men then maybe there could have been more and other people didn't come forward
M: I dunno mm it seems a bit odd that he was raped once before (F: yeah yeah) it's just a bit strange that /er

Challenging Kelley variable
F: what's the relevance of him being raped before
M: well yeah if it's happened five times in six months I'd say (F: yeah yeah) sort of once a month I mean it's not the sort of thing that happens a lot anyway so you'd think it'd be slightly bigger news

Other
M: oh right had been well reported in the local newspapers in the six months before the alleged rape had taken place

When discussing male rape, the first interesting observation is that Kelley's variables do not display such a variety of functions as they do in female rape. Neither are the Kelley variables used overwhelmingly by males to attribute causality to the male victim as they are used to do with the female victim. When making an attribution to the male rape victim using a Kelley variable, these attributions are not overwhelmingly negative as they are in the case of female rape, an observation which extends to both male and female subjects. Overall, the same pattern of Kelley variable use as in discussions of female rape did not prevail. The final analysis was concerned with an examination of the function of each of the Kelley variables separately, i.e. raped before (high consensus/high consistency), other rapes in the area (low distinctiveness). The first two logically point to a stimulus attribution, the third (low distinctiveness) does not.

What actually happens, is that, in the case of female rape, males not only utilize the logic of the variable that the victim has been raped before to make a negative attribution to the victim (as predicted by Kelley's model), but continue to impose the same logic on the variable that other people have also been raped. In the case of male rape, there is a striking omission to impose the same sort of

Table 4. Function of Kelley variables in male rape

	male subjects	female subjects
attribution to victim	9	4
undermine and challenge	6	4
other	8	3

logic on to the variable that other males have been raped. It is the females, in actual fact, who appear to follow Kelley's logic most closely when they make a negative attribution to the victim because they do so primarily with the information that the victim had been raped before. However, it is also necessary to point out that this only happens when they do make a negative attribution to the victim. More often, they put the Kelley variables to other use such as making attributions to the authority responsible for the rape, to the rapist, and of course most frequently of all to undermine and challenge the Kelley variable itself.

Conclusions

In conclusion, males and females appear to differentially evoke Kelley's variables and foreseeability in actual conversation about an alleged rape, as Study 1 showed. Male subjects refer to Kelley's variables more frequently than females, although this significant difference in evoking Kelley's dimensions does not generalize to male rape. Consistent with previous studies, males make more negative attributions to characteristics of the victim than females. They also specifically state that the woman was to blame, that the rape was her fault and that "she was asking for it", more frequently than females. This series of studies also showed that when discussing female rape, male subjects use Kelley's variables (even low distinctiveness which should not lead to a stimulus attribution) to make specifically negative attributions to the rape victim, a finding, which again does not generalize to male rape. Female subjects, consistent with previous studies, do not make as many negative attributions to the female rape victim as males. How do they manage to counter the fact that when discussing female rape with a male, males often tend to make negative attributions to the victim? One way of doing this when discussing rape with a male is to actively challenge and undermine the information implicit in Kelley variables, a finding which brings into question the generality of Kelley's model. This research is really the first to examine Kelley's model in actual conversation. It exposes striking gender differences in attributional reasoning about a depicted rape and gives a hint as to why the crime of rape is still so blatantly under reported.

References

ANTAKI, C., and LEUDAR, I. (1992) From attribution to argumentation: the case of disappearing discourse. **Canadian Psychology, 33,** 594-599

ANTAKI, C., and NAJI, S. (1987) Events explained in conversational "because" statements. **British Journal of Social Psychology, 26,** 119-126

BRIDGES, J., and McGRAIL, C. (1989) Attributions of responsibility for date and stranger rape. **Sex Roles, 21,** 273-286

CALHOUN, L., SELBY, J., and WARING, L. (1976) Social perception of the victim's causal role in rape: an exploratory examination of four factors. **Human Relations, 29,** 517-526

DEITZ, S., LITTMAN, M., and BENTLEY, B. (1984) Attribution of responsibility for rape: the influence of observer empathy, victim resistance and victim attractiveness. **Sex Roles, 10,** 261-280

EDMONDS, E. M., and CAHOON, D. D. (1986) Attitudes concerning crimes related to clothing worn by female victims. **Bulletin of the Psychonomic Society, 24,** 444-446

HOME OFFICE STATISTICAL BULLETIN (1993) Notifiable Offences, England and Wales 1992. Issue 9/93: 28.04.93

KELLEY, H. H. (1967) Attribution theory in social psychology. **Nebraska Symposium on Motivation, 15,** 192-238

L'ARMAND, K., and PEPITONE, A. (1982) Judgements of rape: a study of victim-rapist relationship and victim sexual history. **Personality and Social Psychology Bulletin, 8,** 134-139

LUGINBUHL, J., and MULLIN, C. (1981) Rape and responsibility: how and how much is the victim blamed? **Sex Roles, 7,** 547-559

McARTHUR, L. (1972) The how and what of why: some determinants and consequences of causal attributions. **Journal of Personality and Social Psychology, 22,** 171-193

PALLAK, S. R., and DAVIES, J. M. (1982) Finding fault versus attributing responsibility: using facts differently. **Personality and Social Psychology Bulletin, 8,** 454-459

POLLARD, P. (1992) Judgements about victims and attackers in depicted rapes: a review. **British Journal of Social Psychology, 31,** 307-326

RICHARDSON, D., and CAMPBELL, J. L. (1982) Alcohol and rape: the effect of alcohol on attributions of blame for rape. **Personality and Social Psychology Bulletin, 8,** 468-476

SCROGGS, J. R. (1976) Penalties for rape as a function of victim provocativeness, damage and resistance. **Journal of Applied Social Psychology, 6,** 360-368

SHAVER, K. (1970) Defensive attribution: effects of severity and relevance on the responsibility assigned for an accident. **Journal of Personality and Social Psychology, 14,** 101-113.

Children's views on investigative interviews for suspected sexual abuse

Helen L. Westcott

A small qualitative study was undertaken with 14 children and young people, nine girls and five boys aged 6-18 years who had been interviewed as part of investigations into sexual victimization. They talked about all aspects of their interview and interviewers; most identified both positive and negative experiences. Things that help children in the interview include an explanation of what will happen, choice about who is present, and choice about the interviewer (e.g. gender). Certain interviewer behaviours also help, such as provision of emotional support, a believing stance, and minimizing stress. Factors that do not help young people include a lack of preparation, and evidential requirements dictating the manner in which the interviewees describe their abuse. Unhelpful interviewer responses include the use of age-inappropriate language, a disbelieving stance, and repeated questioning. These findings are discussed in the light of the Criminal Justice Act (1991), the Memorandum of Good Practice, and the tension between evidential versus children's needs in the investigative interview.

Professionals interviewing children suspected of sexual abuse have adopted many different styles and techniques (see Vizard, 1991, for a review). Many of these interviewing styles strive to be child-centred, but as professionals, with personal and professional histories and agendas, it is very difficult to put ourselves in the child's position and imagine what it feels like to be on the receiving end of an investigative interview. This is illustrated by Butler-Slossls well-publicized comments that the child is "a person, and not an object of concern" (1988); and also by the lack of children's perspectives in the interviewing literature. Wattam (1992) is a notable exception in this respect; she conducted a three-year ethnographic study into the disclosure of child sexual abuse (in North-West England) and concluded that:

* disclosure is an organizationally driven process in which the needs of children are typically overlooked and not taken into account;

* children are subjected to organizational constraints without consultation, preparation or anticipation of the consequences;

* children's immediate needs are secondary to evidential needs;

* children do not understand what is going to happen or what is expected of them in the interview situation.

In a Scottish study of short-term and long-term effects of child sexual abuse, Roberts and Taylor (1993) also included direct interviews with children, and incorporated their perspectives in the research report. Some of the children's comments related to their involvement with the investigative and judicial systems, and were predominantly negative in this respect. Roberts and Taylor also highlight the complexity of the children's experiences, and their mixed feelings in reporting and discussing abuse. Overwhelmingly, though, the children and young people in this study felt that speaking out about their abuse was a positive step to take, especially at follow-up interview, and would recommend another abused child to do the same.

This study was therefore prompted by the desire to seek out children's perspectives, and to build upon Wattam's earlier study. If we consider an investigative interview from the child's point of view, there are a number of factors which will affect how well he or she is able to participate, and which will act as facilitators or inhibitors for communication within the interview. For example, these will include:

* *developmental issues*, such as the child's understanding of what an interview is and why it is occurring;

* *cognitive issues*, such as the child's ability to remember details about his or her abuse;

* *personal issues*, such as the fear and embarrassment experienced by the child recalling abuse;

* *motivational issues*, such as the child's desire to participate in an investigative interview, and the degree to which he or she perceives the interview as helpful or relevant to his or her situation;

* *social issues*, such as the rapport or relationship that does or does not build up between the interviewer and the child;

* *structural issues*, such as power relationships which inevitably put the child at a disadvantage (e.g. adult/child, white/black, able bodied/disabled, male/female).

These issues can variously be examined as those pertaining to the interview structure, interviewer, and interviewee (Westcott, 1993a; Young et al., 1987).

In this paper I want to present - necessarily brief - feedback from sexually abused children and young people which illustrates these issues from the child's point of view. Although I shall be stressing several problems these children encountered, this is not to say the interviews they underwent were all bad, or that the interviewers were totally disliked by the children. It is worth acknowledging at the outset the difficulties facing interviewers in investigative interviews, and also the good work done with this group of children that enabled them to participate in my research at all.

Study method

All children and young people were recruited through one NSPCC team, and had been sexually abused (abuse included touching, vaginal and anal intercourse). Recruitment proved exceedingly difficult; over 40 children were approached about the study, but less than half agreed to participate. The first four children to respond acted as pilot interviewees, and 14 children and young people participated in the main study. Children were from different socioeconomic backgrounds, all but one being white European, and all but one being non-disabled. One Chinese girl and one boy with learning difficulties participated. In total, there were nine girls and five boys.

Children ranged in age from six to 18 years at time of research interview, and from five to 16 at investigative interview. Time lapsed between investigative and research interviews ranged from one to four years. All perpetrators were male and known to their victims. The abuse came to light through a disclosure by the child in most cases (n=12). A high number of children in this study (n=11) had seen a prosecution against their perpetrator, which has implications when considering the findings.

A semi-structured interview schedule was used which asked about all aspects of the investigative interview and the interviewer, but did not ask about the sexual abuse perpetrated upon the child (this information was later obtained from case files). In addition to requiring more factual information, such as what happened and who was present, children were asked to provide more subjective responses, for instance, to explain how they felt about the interview. Twelve interviews were conducted at the child's home, and two at NSPCC offices near their homes. With one exception, all were tape-recorded and analysed with the assistance of the Textbase Alpha computer program.

The child's point of view: findings and discussion

These will be presented according to the different types of issues listed above. Obviously, any classification scheme is artificial to a degree, and many issues will inter-relate. Only a small portion of information obtained from the children can be presented here, so I have chosen what seemed to be the most important from the children's point of view. In reproducing excerpts, I have monitored the number of quotes from any one child - several children being of the same age (for example four girls aged 16 years). In discussing the child's point of view, I shall refer to the interview guidance contained in the *Memorandum of Good Practice* (MOGP; Home Office, 1992), although all the investigative interviews here were conducted before the MOGP was implemented.

Developmental issues

One of the biggest problems encountered by children in this study was that of interviewers' language and questioning style. Problems described by children included:

* long, complicated big words;

* long, complicated sentences/questions;

* the way they said things;

* interrupting;

* getting mixed up. For example:

> Words of the question. Difficult topic to talk about and she used quite long words *(Female, 13 years)*.

> Cause if she asked a question, she like went on about it for ages and then she goes, what do you think? I'd completely forgotten what on earth she was going on about *(Female, 16 years)*.

> They kept talking longer then small, so I couldn't keep up with it, and they kept talking a question then a different question before I answered *(Female, 6 years)*.

This difficulty with professionals' language has been noted previously for both defence lawyers and social workers (e.g. Brennan, 1993; Dennett and Bekerian, 1991). Although the MOGP cautions interviewers about using age-inappropriate language, it is worth stressing that not only younger children can have difficulties. If the child is black, and/or is disabled, they may have additional requirements in relation to language.

Another developmental issue relates to the child's understanding of what the interview actually is. In this study, children reported knowing why they were being questioned, although this was not due to any action on the interviewers' part. For most, the investigative interview was something that "just happened" with no warning or preparation. They spoke of interviewers "just turning up", and who "just came to my house". The rushed nature of the interview was viewed unfavourably by several children, who felt it was "too sudden" or "too quick":

> The way they came without us actually knowing, I reckon that was a bit surprising. It didn't help much *(Male, 13 years)*.

Rushing children in this manner does not help them to contribute in a meaningful way, and goes against the spirit of the 1989 Children Act which has also a role in investigative interviews (see *Working Together*, Department of Health, 1991). Under the MOGP, however, it is difficult to see how children could be prepared for the interview, especially as this is one of the least helpful aspects of the Memorandum's guidance (Wattam, 1992).

Cognitive issues

Another difficulty reported by children was in remembering details of their abuse. This is partly a structural issue in relation to the evidential demands put upon children as to how they should describe their abuse within the interview. At a more simple level, however, it was just very difficult to remember, especially as for many children the abuse had been occurring over a number of years.

> Well, they were questioning me about dates and that, and I couldn't remember, that got to me, and times, I mean you don't remember that sort of thing really. How long it went on for an' all that *(Female, 16 years)*.

> Like when [police officer] asked me what were the room like, it was hard to remember, but I tried to, I pictured it in me mind but it kept slipping back out *(Male, 14 years)*.

Again, interviewers may underestimate these problems from the child's point of view, and the MOGP does not appear to anticipate them sufficiently. This may reflect a lack of understanding of the dynamics of sexual abuse, and how factors like time delays can affect children (Wattam, 1992). If a child has an intellectual impairment there may be additional difficulties.

Personal issues

The problem in remembering details linked in with the extreme embarrassment many children and young people felt in talking about their abuse:

> I mean it got easier as I went along but you still had to get down to the very nitty-gritty and actual wording for things like that, and that was very, very embarrassing *(Female, 17 years).*

However, the pressures went further than embarrassment and included fear and nervousness. This resulted from both the formality of the investigative interview, and also from fear of the perpetrator and what would happen now their victimization was out in the open (see also Roberts and Taylor, 1993). It became very apparent that children weighed up a number of likely outcomes from their disclosure, and did not only consider the ramifications for themselves. Thus the genuine relief many children felt as a result of telling was tempered by the negative consequences.

> I did feel relieved afterwards. I knew then from that point whatever I had endured for three years it would finish ... I was scared that I'd have to face me mum, and scared that if ever my stepdad came after me 'cos he'd always said if I told I'd be in trouble *(Female, 17 years).*

> I was feeling better because everyone knew but I felt worse because Grandma and Grandad knew and they were like ignoring the whole subject and he was me Grandma's son, you see, so that made it even worse, you know *(Female, 16 years).*

> Upset about my Grandma, because it would upset her *(Female, 16 years).*

The responsibility appears to rest with the child as "teller", not the adult as "listener" (Jestcott, 1993b); children must, to a large degree, find the resources within themselves to overcome feelings of embarrassment and fear. They also weigh up the likely outcomes for themselves and other people, including the perpetrator (see also Roberts and Taylor, 1993).

For some children, negative consequences overwhelmed the positives to the extent they did not feel good about telling, and said they would not have gone through with the interview, in retrospect.

> Well, worse cause when he comes out he might send somebody after me, cause I was the only one who got it out *(Male, 14 years).*

> It caused so many upsets. If I'd have known ... how it would upset everybody and how much it would have upset me, I don't think I'd have gone through with it, I'd have just kept carrying on how I was *(Female, 17 years).*

Interviewers must put themselves in the position of the child to appreciate the delicate balancing act involved in deciding whether to disclose sexual abuse.

Motivational issues

The lack of preparation for interview noted above could affect the motivation of children to participate in investigative interviews. Additionally, some children just felt that they did not want to talk about their abuse, that it was their own business. Two further issues noted by children in this study were potentially important from the point of view of motivating the child to talk about what had happened: choice/control over where interviews occurred and who was present, and whether or not they felt believed by the interviewers.

Predominantly, young people had been interviewed at their home (n=9), although a police station, school, friend's house and an old people's home were also utilized. Eight children had been seen by joint police and social services investigating teams, and six by police interviewers only. All male interviewees had at least one male interviewer present, and two boys had not had a female interviewer present. All but one female had at least one female interviewer, and two girls had been seen by at least one male professional. (Gender issues are discussed below.)

Only three children had been given any choice over where they were interviewed, although most felt comfortable with the location in which they had been seen. Three children would have preferred to be interviewed elsewhere; for two girls this reflected a desire for privacy from family members (particularly siblings) who could barge in at any time as the interview was conducted at home. Implementation of the MOGP has largely superseded this issue, and most investigative interviews will now be conducted in specialized interviewing suites.

Only two children had not been accompanied by anyone apart from the interviewers during their investigative interview, and one or both parents/step-parents were usually present (n=10). Three young people had been asked who they would like to be present. Five children did not want the other person or persons in the interview, and three had asked them to leave the room. This steeled from a wish for privacy, and also the desire to protect others from hearing their disclosure.

> I would've preferred it if she wasn't there, but I didn't really have a choice ... I suppose because of the details I had to tell the police, I didn't want anybody to know really *(Female, 18 years)*.

> It did matter, because I'm sure if I'd have been with someone I didn't want, I probably wouldn't have said quite honestly and openly about more of these things that went into my statement *(Female, 17 years)*.

> I liked it when Mum and Dad went out. When Mum and Dad was in there I wouldn't talk - I wouldn't say owt. No, I knew it would upset them and they would start crying, and I did not want that *(Female, 16 years)*.

When planning the interview, professionals must discuss, with the child where possible, who is present. This includes who is listening to the interview from behind a one-way screen. Although the MOGP discourages the presence of others in the investigative interview, which is in line with some of the comments above, it may well be that children would benefit from having a supporter present (Moston, 1992), as stated by several children in this study. Again, additional people such as interpreters may be required if the child is disabled, or does not have English as a first language. It is important to recognize that older children and young people are able to contribute meaningfully to decisions about their welfare (Roberts and Taylor, 1993).

Most children in this study felt the interviewers believed them, which was important. Belief was conveyed by the way in which interviewers spoke to the children, were comforting and caring, were helpful and encouraging, and were kind. Young people who did not feel believed mentioned a lack of expression or emotion on behalf of the interviewer, and bullying tactics. One girl in particular found it difficult to decide whether or not she had been believed - an example again of evidential requirements in the investigative interview:

> Well I felt that she believed me but like ... she weren't out to, you know like care for my feelings, she was just out to get this bloke, she just wanted him put away ... But you know like, I don't think she did actually [believe me] 'cos she went over and over everything so she might have been just like not believing me, it felt like she did at the start *(Female, 16 years)*.

Unfortunately, indicators of interviewers' belief, as described by children in this study, would probably not be acceptable under the MOGP, which requires investigative interviews to be conducted in a "neutral atmosphere". This may have both a deleterious effect on the child's welfare and on the quality of his or her evidence (Goodman et al., 1991). The comments of children in this study, and particularly of the girl above, highlight how it is that the process of legal verification may undermine the child's feeling of being believed (Blagg, 1989).

Social issues

Most social issues in this study related to the child's perception of the interviewers. Generally, interviewers were well liked, which was important for the majority of children (one boy said it did not matter). If they did not like the interviewers, children would not talk openly with them:

> Very important because I wouldn't have been able to speak to her if I didn't like her very much and I didn't get on *(Female, 18 years)*.

> If I didn't like her I wouldn't have gone through with it *(Male, 17 years)*.

> Because of the way they were just like blunt or something, I couldn't say the whole story and I never did and haven't now *(Male ,17 years)*.

Obviously this has implications for both the child's emotional wellbeing and the quality of evidence he or she provides. Positive interviewer attributes - there were no differences between police officers and social workers - included the following:

* nice;

* understanding;

* made me laugh;

* friendly;

* kind;

* polite;

* comfortable/comforting;

* not pushy/pressurising;

* sympathetic;

* supportive;

* listened/good to talk to;

* good attitude/way he or she spoke;

* believed me;

* brought his hat and radio;

* not interfering - for example:

    She were kind and understanding. She were polite *(Female, 13 years)*

    I liked him a lot, he tried to make me laugh at times. Yeah it did relax me a lot more, I felt a bit more comfortable in front of him." *(Female, 17 years)*

Children generally could think of more good than bad about their interviewers, but negative interviewer attributes - across police officers and social workers - included the following:

* made it feel unimportant;

* didn't say anything;

* spoke posh;

* snotty;

* spoke to me as if I was just a piece of filth;

* disbelieving;

* blunt;

* chopping and changing my words;

* bored;

* staring;

* treated me younger than I am.

    Don't like the way they sit, at the time I just felt they're not interested, it's not important *(Male, 17 years)*.

    She just sat there really bored, she weren't asking no questions, she just sat there staring at me like that, she weren't even blinking *(Female, 16 years)*.

One of the biggest issues concerned interviewer gender; nine children said it was important, and they all preferred a woman, in line with previous research (Kaplan et al., 1991). This included one girl who had been interviewed by two male police officers. One girl and three boys said interviewer gender was not important, and one girl did not respond. Females were preferred since a man would remind them of their perpetrator and abuse, because the child was "off men" at that time, the child did not trust men, and because women were seen as more understanding and easier to talk to.

    Because if I had a bloke it could remind me *(Female, 16 years)*.

    Because what I was going to, having to explain I think women will understand more I suppose. Men, policemen, I don't think they really care to be honest *(Female, 18 years)*.

    Preferred it to be a woman, because it would be a lot easier to talk to. Well, women understand a man's problem and it's hard for a bloke to understand a man's problem *(Male, 14 years)*.

Young people who did not think interviewer gender was important did not see any difficulties in talking to either men or women. Professionals should not assume however, that victims will not want to talk to male interviewers (Roberts and Taylor, 1993; Westcott, 1993b). All of the child's circumstances (for example, gender, race, culture, disability) must be taken into account when deciding who is the most appropriate person to conduct the interview (Phillips, 1993). It seems the best practice is to offer the child a choice wherever possible.

Structural issues

The final issues highlighted pertain to the interview structure. Most notably here were the requirements about how children should describe their abuse, again reflecting the priority given to evidential needs, and the effective powerlessness of children in the interview situation. As noted above, this also involves developmental and cognitive factors. For example, it may well be simply impossible for the child to remember the specific details required, or to produce them in the desired manner.

> I know I was really scared because I thought you know like it says you got to say it all correct otherwise you get sent to prison ... I was so scared they was saying things like "what was you wearing" and I was thinking "oh my", 'cos it was over a year now ... 'cos I used to change my clothes about five times a day *(Female, 16 years)*.

> I'd talk most of the time but maybe I would sometimes slip and slip something back at the beginning that was supposed to be in my past a bit before what I was talking about at the present and then (police woman) would ask if she wanted to get things clearer *(Female, 17 years)*.

> Because she was like, say like you pick a pin up and then put it in a pile of pins and it's sort of like pick that pin up, you know, and it was like it had to be the way, you know, and I couldn't remember *(Female, 16 years)*.

The last girl was trying to explain how difficult it is to recall specific details of one particular abusive episode distinct from all the others, (i.e. to find one pin from a pile of pins). She thus nicely illustrates again the dynamics of sexual abuse, e.g. repetitions over long periods, and how the investigative interview is designed to meet the needs of professionals rather than the child. Her comments also illustrate the difficulties in distinguishing between particular memories and the memory-script (Nelson, 1986). Other non verbal methods of demonstrating what happened, such as by the use of dolls or props, may facilitate the child's telling, rather than trying to squeeze his/her story into ill-fitting words.

Concluding remarks

The methodological limits of this study must first be noted. It was a small, qualitative piece of research involving a relatively small number of children. Feedback from a larger sample of children, including disabled children and those whose first language is not English, is required. The high proportion of criminal prosecutions and voluntary disclosures by the victims (Sorenson and Snow, 1991) also needs to be considered, although its overall effect is to underline the difficulties children face. If this atypical group of children can report problems, having had belief in their disclosures "concretely" shown by professionals pursuing prosecutions (and achieving convictions in almost all cases), how much more so will the majority of children who see nothing happen beyond an initial interview.

It is too simplistic to divide the children into those who were "all positive" or "all negative". Most recalled both good and bad aspects. Things that help children include the following:

* an explanation of what will happen;

* choice about who is present;

* choice about the interviewer;

* facilitative interviewer behaviours such as the provision of emotional support, the adoption of a believing stance and the minimization of stress.

Things that do not help children include:

* a lack of preparation;

* evidential requirements dictating the manner in which they describe their abuse, and the level of detail desired;

* obstructive interviewer behaviours such as age-inappropriate language, a disbelieving stance and a lack of interest.

In the investigative interviews described by children in this study, evidential needs apparently subjugated children's needs in several areas, a position magnified by the Memorandum (Wattam, 1992; Westcott, 1994). There is something of an adult assumption that information must be available because they want it, and also how they want it. From the child's point of view the task may simply be too difficult for a number of reasons. As a final point, however, it is perhaps worth noting that the majority of children in this study said they would have gone through with the interview, even if they had known what it was going to be like beforehand (in line with Roberts and Taylor's findings). How representative this statement is of all children undergoing investigative interviews, especially those where no prosecution subsequently results, is a matter for further research.

References

BLAGG, H. (1989) Fighting the stereotypes: "ideal" victims in the inquiry process. In H. Blagg, J. A. Hughes and C. Wattam (Eds) **Child Sexual Abuse: Listening, hearing and validating the experiences of children.** Harlow: Longman

BREMAN, M. (1993) A question of language: your quick and easy guide to verbal assault and battery. In W. Stainton-Rogers and M. Worrel (Eds) **Investigative Interviewing with Children.** Milton Keynes: Open University

BUTLER-SLOSS, E. (1988) **Report of the Inquiry into Child Abuse in Cleveland.** London: HMSO

DENNETT, J., and BEKERIAN, D. (1991) Interviewing abused children. **Policing, 7,** 355-360

DEPARTMENT OF HEALTH (1991) **Working Together under the Children Act 1989: A guide to arrangements for inter-agency co-operation for the protection of children from abuse.** London: HMSO

GOODMAN, G. S., BOTTOMS, B., SCHWARTZ-KENNEY, B., and RUDY, L. (1991) Children's testimony about a stressful event: improving children's reports. **Journal of Narrative and Life History, 7,** 69-99

HOME OFFICE (in conjunction with Department of Health) (1992) **Memorandum of Good Practice on Video Recorded Interviews with Child Witnesses for Criminal Proceedings.** London: HMSO

KAPLAN, M. S., BECKER, J. V., and TENKE, C. E. (1991) Influence of abuse history on male adolescent self-reported comfort with interviewer gender. **Journal of Interpersonal Violence, 6,** 1, 3-11

MOSTON, S. (1992) Social support and children's eyewitness testimony. In H. Dent and R. Flin (Eds) **Children as Witnesses.** Chichester: Wiley

NELSON, K. (1986) **Event Knowledge: Structure and function in development.** Hillsdale, NJ: Lawrence Erlbaum

PHILLIPS, M. (1993) Investigative interviewing: issues of race and culture. In W. Stainton-Rogers, and M. Worrel (Eds) **Investigative Interviewing with Children.** Milton Keynes: Open University

ROBERTS, J., and TAYLOR, C. (1993) Sexually abused children and young people speak out. In L. Waterhouse (Ed.) **Child Abuse and Child Abusers: Protection and prevention.** London: Jessica Kingsley

SORENSON, T. K., and SNOW, B. (1991) How children tell: the process of disclosure in child sexual abuse. **Child Welfare, 70,** 1, 3-15

VIZARD, E. (1991) Interviewing children suspected of being sexually abused: a review of theory and practice. In C. R. Hollin and K. Howell (Eds) **Clinical Approaches to Sex Offenders and their Victims.** Chichester: Wiley

WATTAM, C. (1992) **Making A Case in Child Protection.** Harlow: Longman

WESTCOTT, H. L. (1994) **One Year On: Professionals' concerns about the Memorandum of Good Practice.** London: NSPCC

WESTCOTT, H. L. (1993a) Interviewing children in an investigative context. In Department of Health funded training and resource pack **Abuse and Children who are Disabled.**

WESTCOTT, H. L. (1993b) **Abuse of Children and Adults with Disabilities.** London: NSPCC

YOUNG, J. G., O'BRIEN, J. D., GUTTERMAN, E. M., and COHEN, P. (1987) Research on the clinical interview. **Journal of the American Academy of Child and Adolescent Psychiatry, 26,** 5, 613-620

The Cognitive Interview and suggestibility

Rebecca Milne, Ray Bull, Gunter Koehnken and Amina Memon

To establish more fully the use of the Cognitive Interview (CI) it must be shown that the CI does not increase witness suggestibility. Previous research (Geiselman et al., 1986) found that the CI decreased suggestibility to leading and misleading questions but only when the CI mnemonics were presented before these question types. Studies of children imply that sometimes they may be particularly vulnerable to suggestion. This study investigated the extent to which the CI assisted children to resist the effects of leading and misleading questions (both script consistent and inconsistent questions). Eighty-five children aged from eight to ten years viewed a video recording of a magic show. A day later each child was individually interviewed, using either the CI or a structured interview. A (mis)leading questionnaire was presented either before or after their interview. Results are presented and discussed.

Psychologists in the USA have developed a witness interviewing procedure, the Cognitive Interview (CI), based upon extant psychological research, concerning the retrieval of information from memory. The principal advocates of this technique, Ed Geiselman and Ron Fisher, claim that the CI can increase both the quantity and quality of information elicited from an eyewitness without increasing errors or confabulations.

According to the Criminal Justice Act (1991) children below the age of 8 are now seen as competent witnesses, thus, the number of child witnesses is going to increase and so, there is a need for non-suggestible interview strategies (Milne and Bull, 1994). How effective is the CI with child witnesses? Results have been mixed. Geiselman and Paedilla (1988) found that the CI increases accurate recall by 21 per cent. However, Koehnken et al. (1991) found a similar increase in accurate recall, but also an increase in errors with the CI. And, Memon et al. (1992) found no recall differences between the CI and a standard interview (control, SI). Thus, the first aim of the study was to assess the relative effectiveness of the CI in use with children.

It must be shown that the CI is non-suggestible. One study (Geiselman et al., 1985) found that the CI decreases the effects of suggestion with adults, but only when the suggestion was presented after the CI mnemonic techniques. Studies of children imply that they may be particularly vulnerable to suggestion (Baxter, 1990) and so, the second study aim examined the extent to which the CI assisted children to resist the effects of leading and misleading questions (both script consistent and script inconsistent).

Method

Design

The design was a $2 \times 2 \times 2 \times 3$ factorial design. The CI versus Standard Interview (control, SI) condition was of between Ss design, as was the (mis)leading questions that were presented before or after the interview. The rest of the conditions were of within-subjects design and were incorporated into a suggestibility questionnaire. These consisted of script consistent versus script inconsistent (mis)leading question types as defined by an independent group aged between seven and 11, and, finally, neutral, leading versus misleading question types.

Participants

Eighty-four children aged between eight and nine years, 41 boys and 43 girls, took part in the study.

Interviewers

The SI interviewers were all undergraduates, three females and one male, with ages ranging from 19 to 24 years (mean = 20.5 years). The CI group consisted of one female undergraduate and three male graduates. Their ages ranged from 19 to 25 years (mean = 22 years).

Training

All interviewers participated in two four-hour training sessions, which consisted of lectures (explaining the underlying theory), examples, practices and role-playing with video feedback, and personal comments from the trainers. The CI and SI interviewers were trained separately and throughout the study it was ensured that the two groups did not know that they were trained differently.

Apparatus and materials

Stimulus. The video recording depicted a magic show that lasted nine minutes. Its theme was chosen to be not only of interest to children, but also being full of action, person and object details.

Misleading questionnaire. This consisted of explicit leading and misleading questions (both script consistent and inconsistent) similar to those defined by Rudy and Goodman (1991). This type of questioning was chosen as some interviewers have been criticized for using this questioning style when interviewing children (Bull, 1993). The questionnaire also included filler non-leading or neutral questions. The question total was 20 and contained eight leading (four script consistent, four script inconsistent), eight misleading (four script consistent, four script inconsistent), and four neutral question types. There were equal numbers of correct yes and no answers to these questions to counteract response biasing.

Procedure

Groups of eight children were shown the video recording of the magic show. A day later each child was randomly assigned to one of the four conditions and individually interviewed. Each audio-taped interview was then transcribed into a written format and recall was evaluated in terms of correct, incorrect and confabulated details.

Scoring procedure

The magic show video recording was put into a written format and the details were categorized into four groups; person, action, object and surrounding. Per "detail group" an exhaustive list containing all the available details was drawn up with the appropriate scores next to each specific detail. Instructions used by interviewers were quantified.

The children's free report, response after "remember more" prompt, responses to questioning, and reverse order recall (CI) or second recall attempt (SI) responses were coded and scored separately with only new information being evaluated. Each recalled detail was analysed with respect to being correct, incorrect, or a confabulation within the detail categories. A piece of information was coded as incorrect if the detail was discrepant with the respective detail in the film (e.g. red jumper instead of black jumper; an error concerning colour). If a detail was mentioned that was not present in the film it was coded as a confabulation. Total correct, incorrect and confabulated details were thus calculated. With regard to the (mis)leading questionnaire each child's response to each question was scored as being (mis)led, not (mis)led, "don't know" and error. Non-leading/neutral questions were scored for accuracy.

Results: interview results

Overall recall

Children interviewed with the CI recalled significantly more accurate details than those interviewed with an SI (t=2.675, df=82, p<0.009). There were no significant differences in the amount of errors or confabulated details recalled (see Figure 1).

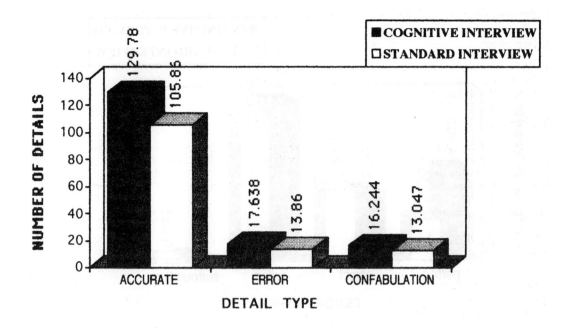

Figure 1. CI and SI recall differences

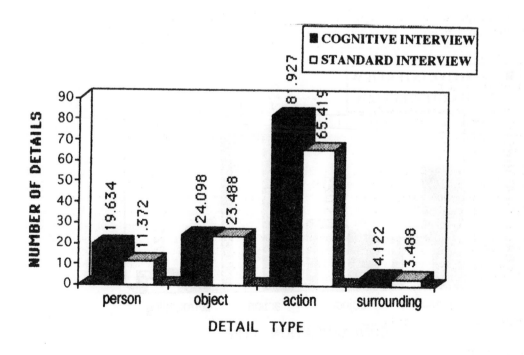

Figure 2. CI and SI accurate recall of detail types

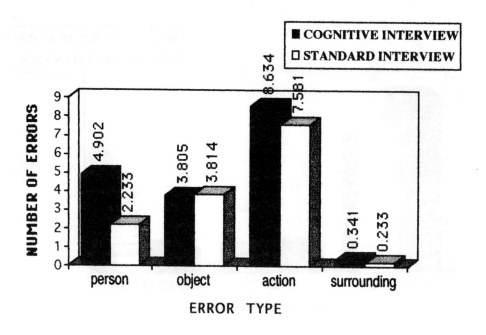

Figure 3. Number of error detail types per interview condition

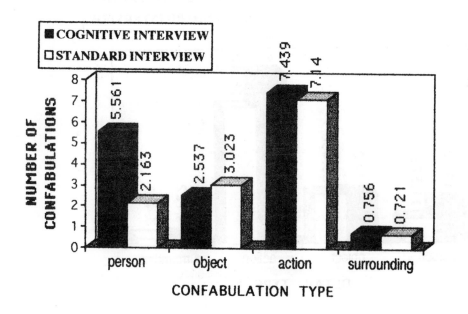

Figure 4. Confabulation type per interview condition

Accurate recall of detail types

Children in the CI group significantly recalled more person (t=6.201, df=82, p<0.0001) and action (t=2.473, df=82, p<0.0155) accurate details (see Figure2).

Error detail types

The CI group of children made significantly more person errors (t=4.947, df=82,p0.0001) than those in the SI group (see Figure 3).

Confabulation detail types

Similarly, there is a significant difference between interview type in the number of confabulated person details mentioned, with the CI group making more confabulations (t=4.118, df=82, p<0.0001; see Figure 4).

Reliability

The reliability of the information (i.e. the proportion of correct details relative to the total number of details reported) did not vary as a function of interview type (80.7 per cent for the CI and 79.6 per cent for the SI, respectively).

Results: suggestibility data

Neutral questions

In order to establish "baseline" similarity neutral (control) questions were examined. No significant differences for interview type or presentation type were found with this variable.

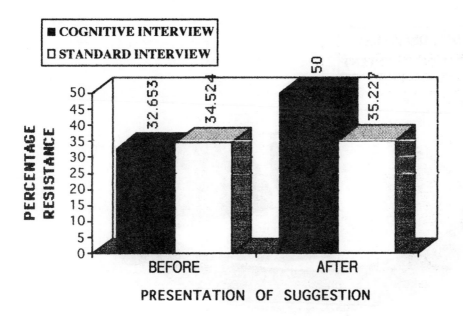

Figure 5. Percentage resistance to misleading questions presented before or after the interview

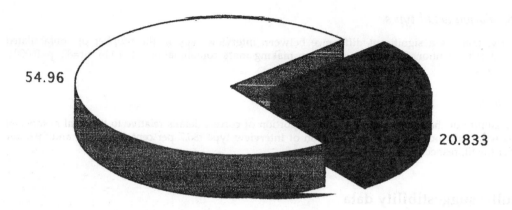

Figure 6. Percentage resistance to script consistent and script inconsistent misleading questions

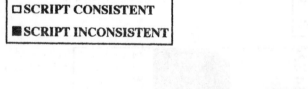

Figure 7. Percentage resistance to script consistent and script inconsistent leading questions

Misleading questions

Using a "one within and two between" repeated measures ANOVA for interview type, presentation type and instruction usage (this latter variable is not discussed in this paper) it was found that resistance to misleading questions was significantly higher after than before a CI interview ($F_{1,80}$ = 6.158, p<0.0175). No such effects were found with the ANOVA for the SI group. Also, resistance was significantly higher with script inconsistent misleading questions than with script consistent misleading questions ($F_{1,80}$=80.776, p<0.0001). No significant interaction was found between presentation of the misleading questions (before versus after the interview) and script type (inconsistent versus consistent; see Figures 5 and 6 respectively).

Leading questions

Resistance was significantly higher with script consistent leading questions than with script inconsistent leading questions ($F_{1,80}$ = 7.288, p<0.0102; see Figure 7).

Discussion

The CI enhances children's accurate recall of person and action details (which may well be forensically relevant to a real police investigation). However, the CI also increases the recall of person errors and confabulations. With respect to suggestion the CI increases children's resistance to misleading questions but, only when these questions are presented after the CI. This has important implications as the CI not only increases recall but it also can be deemed non-suggestible. Finally, it has been shown that it is important to differentiate script consistent and inconsistent question types as children react differently to these types of questions in a suggestion context. This distinction could account for the mixed results found in the classic studies examining children and suggestibility which often do not take this script factor into account.

References

BAXTER, J. S. (1990) The suggestibility of child witnesses: a review. **Applied Cognitive Psychology, 4,** 393-407

BULL, R. (1993) Innovative techniques for the questioning of child witnesses especially those who are young and those with learning disabilities. In M. Zaragoza (Ed.) **Memory, Suggestibility and Eyewitness Testimony in Children and Adults**

GEISELMAN, R. E., FISHER, R. P., MacKINNON, D. P., and HOLLAND, H. L. (1985) Eyewitness memory enhancement in the police interview: cognitive retrieval mnemonics versus hypnosis. **Journal of Applied Psychology, 70,** 401-412

GEISELMAN, R. E., and PADILLA, J. (1988) Interviewing child witnesses with the cognitive interview. **Journal of Police Science And Administration, 16,** 4, 236-242

KOHNKEN, G., FINGER, M., and NITSCHKE, N. (1991) Statement validity analysis and the cognitive interview with child witnesses. Unpublished manuscript. Germany: University of Kiel

MEMON, A., CRONIN, O., EAVES, R., and BULL, R. (1992) The cognitive interview and child witnesses. Paper presented at the Second Annual DCLP Conference

MILNE, R., and BULL, R. (1994) Improving witness recall: The cognitive interview and the legal profession. **Journal of Child Law,** April

RUDY, L., and GOODMAN, G. S. (1991) Effects of participation on children's reports: implications for children's testimony. **Developmental Psychology, 27,** 4, 527-538

A study of reported satisfaction with differentially aggressive computer games amongst incarcerated young offenders

Patricia A. Hind

The research investigated the satisfaction reported by young offenders following the playing of two interactive computer games requiring identical skills, but involving differing levels of perceived aggression and planning for successful completion. The methodology involved adminstering questionnaires to 72 incarcerated young offenders aged between 15 and 18. Forty of these had a record of violent offending, whilst the remainder did not. A control group of some 30 young, male non-offenders was also used. In addition to the questionnaire, a measure of self esteem was obtained, and biographical data was recorded. Subjects were asked to play two short computer games, and to rate their satisfaction with both. The results indicated that the computer game which involved pattern planning to achieve success was reported as being less satisfying than that which simply required the "destruction" of objects. Further, between group differences were obtained on game satisfaction scores, and self esteem scores.

This study was undertaken as a pilot study, looking at the causes and correlates of juvenile crime.

Much earlier work has established links between childhood and adolescent experiences and offending or delinquent behaviour. Major reviews, such as Loeber and Southhammer-Loeber (1986, 1987) and Snyder and Patterson (1987) point to the role of individual experiences, and learning, in predicting and explaining criminal behaviour. Factors such as particular patterns of child rearing, often in association with early antisocial behaviour have been shown to be predictive of criminality. Indeed, "common sense" held, for many years, that discipline, administered by some external authority, be it parent, teacher, policeman, vicar or even post office lady, was the only way to control the antisocial behaviours of the young. The assumption that children must be taught to behave in an acceptable manner underpins most social structures. The further assumption being made that, once a child has "learnt" what is acceptable, then internalization of this knowledge will lead to self control, and "legal" or "civilized" behaviour.

Consequently, much research has already been carried out into the application of Social Learning Theory (SLT). Behavioural methods are used to meet management needs, and to identify behavioural targets in the treatment of young offenders.

Thus, whilst accepting Bandura's (1996) statement that "genetic factors affect behavioural potentialities. Both experiential and physiological factors interact ...", this paper focuses on the importance of more specific learning in determining individual criminal potential. This is largely because the rising levels, particularly of violent crime, are more likely to be associated with changing social experience than changing genetic structures - recent Home Office statistics indicate that violent crime rose by 3.8 per cent in 1993, recorded rapes rose by 12 per cent, whilst robberies increased by 10 per cent.

A disturbing feature of these figures is the associated decrease in age of offending juveniles, particularly in "headline" cases such as the Jamie Bulger murder; other instances can be quoted of violent crimes being committed by those too young to be dealt with by the courts.

A possible area in which to search for a link between these three factors (the importance of learning and individual experience, the rise in violent crime, and the decreasing ages of offenders), is obviously the world of computer games. The technological revolution which has made computer games available to all is relatively recent (in 1972 a computerized table tennis game called *PONG* was the first to become available), thus, here we have a contemporary, novel form of experience available to most members of the population, and becoming more common as the years progress. The UK home computer market has enjoyed an unprecedented "explosion" in recent years, to such an extent that the Economist Intelligence Unit has predicted that by 1995, one in four boys will own a handheld game. There is current debate as to whether the effects of computer games are negative or positive, but this study specifically explores whether a link may be made between computer games, learning experiences and juvenile crime. There are certainly grounds for investigating a possible link. Research (Graham, 1988; Griffiths, 1991a) indicates that computer games are mostly played by male adolescents - the target group when considering juvenile crime.

Analysis of the research investigating the link between computer games and aggression or violence, reveals few conclusive findings. For example, Bowman and Rotter (1983) argue that the violence represented within a computer game in fact offers a release of aggressive emotions, and therefore fulfils a useful and beneficial function. Other researchers (Zimbardo, 1982) have reported increased levels of violence in children after having played computer games. In relation to television a similar picture emerges, Wilson and Hermstein (1985) point out that research on the effects on individuals of watching violence on TV explains those effects either in terms of catharsis, or disinhibition, or modelling. However, Messner (1986) found that aggregate levels of exposure to TV were inversely related to rates of violent crime. However, the majority of studies point to the conclusion that viewing violence does increase interpersonal aggression, particularly in young boys. This argues against aggression catharsis and for the view that aggression is a drive.

Obviously it is incorrect to imply that all TV is violent, and similarly, it is incorrect to imply that all computer games are violent. However, it is true to say that much aggressive imagery is used in computer games. Provenzo (1991) reported that 40 out of 47 analysed games involved violence, and he concluded that such games encouraged violence by conditioning children to view the world in the way it is represented on the computer screen.

The difference between computer game and TV violence lies obviously in the interactive nature of the relationship between the juvenile and the computer game. Players have to make a voluntary, discriminatory response to the screen in order for the game to progress. These responses may or may not be correct, but if they are, they will be reinforced by progression through the game, and high scores. Research on this relationship is, at present, scarce, and has focused on short-term behavioural effects. This study has taken a different approach and considers the reinforcing effects of computer games, from a learning perspective. The model proposed is not that of aggression as a drive, but that the motivational base is that of the need to succeed. The game player is motivated simply by the positive feedback he receives about his performance when his responses to the game are "correct".

It is hypothesized that, given the violent content of many games, success within those games is achieved by the destruction of, or aggression towards, designated "enemies" or "victims". Success, or high scores in any walk of life are found to be reinforcing, according to learning principles, and computer games are unlikely to be different in this regard. Thus, the more enemies destroyed, the more successful the player has been, and thus the more rewarding, or reinforcing he will find the experience. Further, this success is directly attributable to the player's own performance or behaviour. So, a violent act, albeit symbolic violence, has resulted in a positive outcome for the player. To extend the operant learning principles derived from Skinner (1938) as any behaviour followed by reinforcement is strengthened, it is in this regard that game playing is potentially addictive. Learning theory would also predict that successful, (self or peer) rewarded behaviours may generalize across situations, and it is here, through direct reinforcement of symbolic violence, that there may be a link between game playing and violent behaviours. Indeed, it may be argued that the most potent of reinforcement schedules, interval schedules, are those operating within the context of a computer game.

Further implications of the reinforcing potential of computer game playing are that "instant" reinforcement is part of the package. Success or failure on games is immediately apparent, and again, this expectation of immediate gratification may generalize to non-game playing behaviour. The long-term planning upon which success in most walks of life depend, and which may therefore be assumed to be associated with a positive self concept, or self esteem, will be independent of this type of reinforcement. Self esteem may also be linked into this model from a different perspective. Averill (1983) has suggested that loss of self esteem may be a common cause of aggression.

In a pilot study, undertaken at Feltham YOI, convicted and remand prisoners were asked to play two different computer games. One game involved the destruction of successively presented missiles, whilst the other involved the selective placement of geometric shapes. Unwanted shapes were "shot away". In order to identify unwanted shapes a degree of planning and forward thought were required. The study generated the following hypotheses:

Hypothesis 1: that reported preference for computer games representing violent actions will be correlated with violent behaviours.

Hypothesis 2: that greater degrees of familiarity with the instant reinforcement offered by computer games would be negatively correlated with long-term planning behaviours.

Hypothesis 3: that long-term planning behaviours would be positively correlated with self esteem scores.

Hypothesis 4: that for all the above hypotheses, there would be differences between groups of incarcerated young offenders, and a control group of non-offenders.

Methodology

Subjects

Three groups of subjects were initially identified:

Group 1 - pupils at Dulwich College School. All were full-time boarders and had no convictions for criminal behaviour (n=31, average age = 17.2 years). 22 per cent of this group were from single parent families.

Group 2 - inmates of Feltham Young Offenders Institution, either on remand or having been convicted. The members of this group acknowledged no crimes of violence (n=33, average age = 16.7 years). 66 per cent of this group were from single parent families.

Group 3 - inmates of FYOI, either on remand or having been convicted. All the members of this group acknowledged convictions at some time of at least one violent crime. The criteria for violence was set at ABH, robbery, GBII, murder or rape (n=32, average age 16.6 years). 86 per cent of this group were from single parent families,

Total number of subjects = 96

Measures used

All subjects were asked to play two computer games. These were presented through the Super Nintendo system, to a TV screen. The games were the "standard" games purchased with the system, and were therefore fairly basic in terms of graphics.

Each game required identical skills. The game labelled *Lazerblazer* presented missiles traversing the screen which the subject had to shoot to destroy. The game labelled *Blastris* presented geometric shapes traversing the screen; the subject had to "shoot away" those shapes which would not fit into a specified pattern.

The "shots" for both games were made using a "Lazergun" issued with the Nintendo system, requiring the subject to actively press a trigger to shoot the target. The Nintendo system used was relatively new, and no subjects reported having used an identical one before. Subjects were allowed to play each game for a period of between 5 to 7 minutes, and game sessions were terminated at an appropriate point, i.e. when a "level" or a "game" had been completed.

Having played each game, subjects were asked to rate their enjoyment of the game on a 5 point scale, and to comment on any features of the game they found particularly enjoyable or otherwise, and, where possible, give reasons.

Subjects were also required to complete the adult form of the Coopersmith (1991) Self Esteem Inventory. Independent completion of the inventory was not always possible for groups 2 and 3, some of whom had literacy problems. The inventory was read to those subjects.

Data was collected regarding the following variables:

* Number of hobbies actively pursued.

* Specific plans for the future.

* Amount of time (hours per week) spent playing computer games.

Subjects were asked to indicate how many hours, on average, they spent playing computer games, either at home, or in arcades, or both. The estimate referred to times when the boys were able to voluntarily determine how to spend their time, i.e. for the Feltham boys, this meant when they were "out", and for the Dulwich boys, weekends and\or holidays. This variable was "gameplay".'

In addition to the above measures, biographical data was obtained in relation to the subject's family structure, and records of offending behaviour. Subjects were asked how many convictions they had, what the offences were, and, specifically, how many convictions they had for offences of violence. The order of presentation of measures was random.

Results

Results will be presented in order, to correspond to the hypotheses.

Initial inspection of the results indicated that the scores of groups 2 and 3 were too similar to merit separate analysis. The information on which allocation to either of these groups was based was self report data, notoriously unreliable in situations such as this. The scores from these groups were therefore collapsed and all subjects from Feltham YOI were treated as being one group.

After initial analyses, the scores from two games *Lazerblazer* and *Blastris* were also collapsed to form a new score, representing satisfaction levels with both games. This variable was called "duogame".

Hypothesis 1: that reported preference for computer games representing violent actions will be correlated with offending behaviours.

Table 1 shows the distribution of the satisfaction scores for the games *Lazerblazer*, *Blastris*, and the combined score "duogame". As can be seen, the pattern of preference is similar for the two groups, however, satisfaction rates are higher overall for the Feltham group.

Paired *t* tests on the *Lazerblazer/Blastris* scores revealed a significant difference for the Feltham group (p=.0389, significant at .01). A significant correlation was revealed for the Dulwich group on these scores (0.3946, signnificant at .01).

A 2x2 ANOVA, for the Feltham group, indicated a significant main effect of Duogame (p<.023), with those expressing higher satisfaction with both games reporting higher numbers of previous offences.

Regression equations were unable to significantly predict numbers of previous offences. However, the beta values of *Lazerblazer* scores in all the equations analysed were consistently the most influential scores.

Hypothesis 1 was generally supported.

Hypothesis 2: that greater degrees of familiarity with the instant reinforcement offered by computer games would be negatively correlated with long-term planning behaviours.

Table 2 illustrates the very significant difference between the groups as to numbers of plans. This difference was significant at the .001 level.

There were also significant between group differences on overall gameplay scores (significant at .001). Table 3 illustrates that although a similar frequency distribution pattern is found for both groups, when hours per week are examined, the figures these distributions represent are very different.

Table 1. Game satisfaction scores

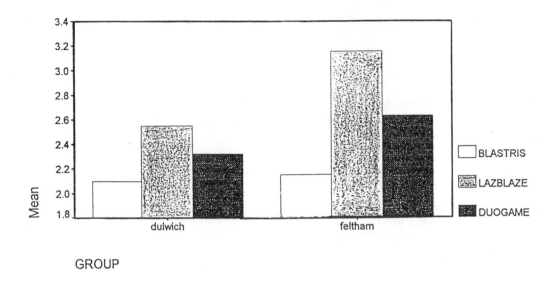

BLASTRIS
LAZBLAZE
DUOGAME

Mean

dulwich   feltham

GROUP

Table 2.

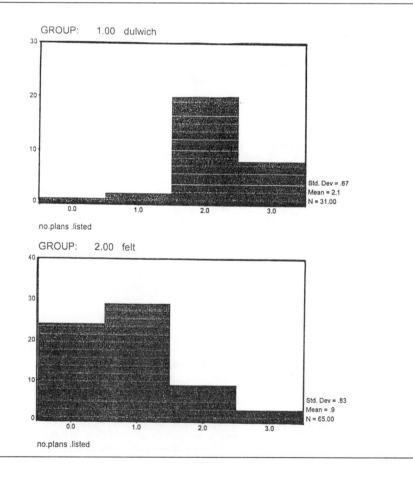

GROUP: 1.00   dulwich

Std. Dev = .67
Mean = 2.1
N = 31.00

no.plans .listed

GROUP: 2.00   felt

Std. Dev = .83
Mean = .9
N = 65.00

no.plans .listed

Table 3.

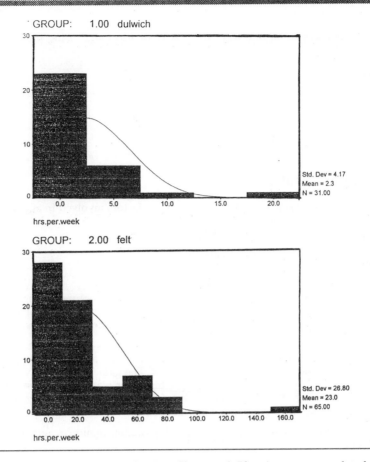

For the Feltham group (2/3) scores on both the *Lazerblazer* and *Blastris* games correlated with the plans variable (significant level .05). This finding is, in fact, in the opposite direction to that predicted by Hypothesis 2.

No interaction was found between plans, and either gameplay or duogame, thus this hypothesis was not supported.

Hypothesis 3: that long-term planning would be positively correlated with self esteem scores.

For the Dulwich group (1), self esteem scores were negatively correlated with the collapsed duogame scores. There was no corresponding correlation for the Feltham group.

Significant differences (.001) were found for both groups using matched pairs *t* tests on the pairing of plans\self esteem scores. A significant difference was found between both groups on overall self esteem scores (significant at .01).

Although a regression equation was unable to predict overall duogame satisfaction scores, the self esteem score was consistently the least contributing factor, for both groups.

These results offer some support for Hypothesis 3.

Hypothesis 4: that for all the earlier hypotheses, there would be a difference between groups of incarcerated young offenders and a control group of non-offenders.

Significant differences, using *t* tests, were found between groups 1 and 2\3 on the following variables:

	Significant level
Number of hobbies listed	.001
Hours per week playing computer games	.001
Number of future plans listed	.001
Self esteem	.01
Satisfaction with the *Lazerblazer* game	.01

Significant differences using one way ANOVA were also found using the original (3) groups, on the following variables:

Self esteem	.05
Gameplay	.01
Hobbies	.001
Plans	.001

These results offer support for Hypothesis 4.

Discussion of results

Bandura (1973a, 1973b) suggests that there are 3 key factors involved in aggression:

* the acquisition of the aggressive behaviour;

* the process of instigation of the aggression;

* the conditions which maintain tile aggression.

Social learning theory argues that acquisition of behaviour occurs through the process of learning, either through direct experience or by observation. There is empirical evidence to suggest that aggressive behaviour can be acquired through direct reinforcement (Hayes, 1980), and by observation (Bandura, 1973b).

It is the thesis of this paper that both methods of acquisition are given the opportunity to be effective, and to interact, via the playing of computer games. The game player is given direct reinforcement for his behaviour by noting his success in hitting a target, or watching a score count rise. He is also able to observe, on the computer screen, the results of the behaviour of the animated characters depicted in the game, who are usually involved in aggressive interaction.

It is also possible that computer game playing might reinforce aggression through 3 types of reinforcement:

* external reinforcement, by peer group competition to play on higher "levels", or to achieve higher scores.

* vicarious reinforcement, through witnessing the success of the aggression of the game characters.

* self-reinforcement, through achieving success on the game by actively initiating an aggressive act, translated into game playing. It is important to note the interactive nature of computer game playing, and to reiterate that success or failure is directly attributable to some voluntary, and discriminatory act on the part of the player.

It is acknowledged that there have been criticisms of the application of the learning theory perspective to this field. Siann (1985) points out that much research of this genre is too narrow, positivist and unrealistic in its approach. It is felt that these criticisms do not apply to this paper, addressing itself, as it does, to the underlying principles by which some generalized aggressive behaviours may be acquired.

Before examining the results, some major methodological weaknesses must be acknowledged.

Firstly, the issue of self report data is obviously a critical one. Much of the information in this study was obtained by subjects who may well have believed they had a vested interest in distorting their reports. Each subject was assured that the research was an independent university study, and that the information revealed was entirely confidential. However, particularly with regard to records of past offending, numbers of crimes of violence, and even perhaps reported pastimes or plans, subjective report on these matters is unlikely to have been reliable.

Secondly, some of the measures used were crude and simplistic. For example, asking subjects how many hours they spent playing computer games, or to list their plans for the future, were obviously not sophisticated or subtle ways of eliciting data. However, the same measures were applied to all subjects, and it is difficult to see how more sophisticated or more subtle data could be gleaned. For future research, reliability measures of this sort of data could be built in, for example, detailed knowledge of game content could be checked against reported time spent playing games.

Thirdly, the games used in this study were also relatively unsophisticated and unexciting, compared with others readily available today. It may well have been that more stimulating games would have produced more clear cut results, particularly with those subjects whose previous game playing experience was extensive. Many subjects asked for particular other games to be included in the study, notably *Streetfighter 2*. However, the two games used did represent similar levels of skill, and stimulation, and were therefore considered appropriate as a basis for comparison.

Given the above limitations, the results of the study were encouraging.

Hypothesis 1: reported preference for computer games representing violent actions will be correlated with violent behaviours.

If this hypothesis had specified "offending behaviours" it would have been found to be generally supported, in that the offender group (groups 2\3) showed a preference for the more violent game, that was not shared by the control group. Further, when overall satisfaction with the games presented was looked at, those offenders with higher satisfaction scores appeared to be those with the highest number of previous offences.

Hypothesis 2: that greater degrees of familiarity with the instant reinforcement offered by computer games would be negatively correlated with long-term plans.

There was little direct evidence for this hypothesis in terms of identifiable interactions, however, there was noted a significant difference between the groups in terms of number of plans listed, and in terms of experience of game playing. It may be that the weaknesses in the measures used masked any possible interactions here. The positive association found between the scores on plans and both the *Lazerblazer* and *Blastris* scores for the Feltham group may have been a chance finding, or may represent a flaw in the scoring of the plans variable.

Hypothesis 3: that "plans" would be positively correlated with self esteem scores.

"Self esteem" refers to the judgement of worth a person habitually makes with regard to him or herself. It indicates a judgemental process, and the extent to which individuals believe themselves to be competent, significant, worthy or successful. Whilst the criteria for success, or worth may vary across populations, the Coopersmith Self Esteem Inventory, as an attitude measure, has been used with a variety of normative samples, and results have not been found to be significantly different. The assumption underlying the measure is that self esteem is significantly associated with personal satisfaction and effective functioning. The framework of this paper holds that the satisfactions or reinforcements obtained, as listed earlier in this discussion, and success on game playing being seen as a measure of effective functioning, would link self esteem with computer game playing.

Again, although inter-relationships between variables could not be clarified, there was clearly a difference between groups on both these variables. The negative relationship for the control group on the pairing of self esteem and overall game satisfaction scores fits the general framework of this paper, as does the significant difference for both groups between plans and self esteem. However, this relationship may have been compounded by a relationship between overall satisfaction and success with computer game playing leading to enhanced self esteem. Although the present data could not clarify this relationship, an area for future research is suggested here. No measure of degree of success, or expertise with computer games was taken here, but future research could explore this area.

Hypothesis 4: that differences would be found between the groups.

This hypothesis was well supported, with particular clusters of differences being noted, linking the variables self esteem, gameplay, hobbies and plans. It should be pointed out here that the "hobbies" variable was unable to inform the hypothesis of this paper. However, it showed a similar responding pattern to the variable "plans". Qualitatively, the information gathered on the reported hobbies of the subjects was interesting. Virtually 100 per cent of the control group reported a variety of sporting activities as hobbies. Approximately 80 per cent of the Feltham group reported music, or "raving" as a hobby, with only a minority referring to sport. However, this is probably due to the circumstances in which the subjects were living, and future research should specify information on voluntary pastimes when "outside" or "on holiday".

Conclusion

Despite methodological problems, this study did not refute the theoretical framework proposed. Sufficient support was found for the hypothesis to indicate that computer game playing may be linked to offending behaviour, via individual and vicarious reinforcement, to warrant further research. It is suggested that such future studies should address the issues of level of violence represented in computer games, peer group involvement, and personal correlates of immediate and long-term reinforcement.

References

AVERILL, J. R. (1983) Studies on anger and aggression: implications for theories of emotion. **American Psychologist, 38**

BANDURA, A. (1973a) **Aggression: A Social Learning Analysis**. Englewood Cliffs, NJ: Prentice Hall

BANDURA, A. (1973b) Social learning theory of aggression. In J. F. Kautson (Ed.) **The Control of Aggression: Implications from Basic Research**. Chicago, ILL: Aidine

BANDURA, A. (1986) **Social Foundations of Thought and Action**. Englewood Cliffs, NJ: Prentice Hall

BOWMAN, R. P., and ROTTER, J. C. (1983) Computer games: friend or foe? **Elementary School Guidance and Counselling, 18**, 25-34

COOPERSMITH, S. (1991) **Self Esteem Inventories**. Consulting Psychologists Press, Inc.

GRAHAM, J. (1988) **Amusement Machines: Dependency and Delinquency**. Home Office Research Study No.101. London: HMSO

GRIFFITHS, M. D. (1991a) Amusement machine playing in childhood and adolescence: a comparative analysis of video games and fruit machines. **Journal of Adolescence, 14**, 53-73

HAYES, S. C., RINCOVER, A., and VOLOSIN, D. (1980) Variables influencing the acquisition and maintenance of aggressive behaviour: modeling versus sensory reinforcement. **Journal of Abnormal Psychology, 89**, 254-262

LOEBER, R., and STOUTHAMMER-LOEBER, M. (1986) Family factors as correlates and predictors of juvenile conduct problems and delinquency. In M. Tonry and N. Morris (Eds) **Crime and Justice: An Annual Review of Research, 7**, 29-150. Chicago: University of Chicago Press

MESSNER, S. R. (1986) Television and violent crime: an aggregate analysis. **Social Problems, 33**, 218-235

PROVENZO, E. (1991) **Video Kids**. Cambridge, MA: Harvard University Press

SIANN, G. (1985) **Accounting for Aggression: Perspectives on Aggression and Violence**. London: Allen & Unwin

SKINNER, B. F. (1938) **The Behaviour of Organisms**. New York: Appleton Century Crofts

SNYDER, J., and PATTERSON, G. R. (1987) Family interaction and delinquent behaviour. In H. C. Quay (Ed.) **Handbook of Juvenile Delinquency**, 216-243. New York: Wiley

WILSON, J. Q., and HERRENSTEIN, R. J. (1985) **Crime and Human Nature**. New York: Simon and Schuster

ZIMBARDO, P. (1982) Understanding psychological man: a state of the science report. **Psychology Today, 16**, 15

Staff perceptions of illicit drug use within a Special Hospital

Helen Liebling and Mick McKeown

This paper presents the results of a survey of staff perceptions of issues related to illicit drug use amongst patients within a special hospital. The issues examined were: the nature and extent of drug related problems, current management strategies and their perceived efficacy, suggestions for improved management strategy, and identification of staff training needs. Data was collected utilizing a questionnaire distributed to all patient care team members and representatives of disciplines working in off ward areas. The response was approximately 40 per cent. Analysis of the returns suggests that staff concerns are largely focused on issues around the supply of drugs. Importantly, a significant level of ignorance regarding illicit drugs and their usage was revealed, indicating a need for a co-ordinated training programme. A review of literature suggests that future strategies should not be solely directed towards supply restriction. Recommendations were made that attention to demand conditions and a harm reduction policy would encompass the best approach.

Ashworth Hospital is one of the four Special Hospitals in the UK, providing care and therapy in conditions of maximum security for 527 male patients and 66 female patients. At the time of conducting this survey the hospital comprised 29 wards, each having a multi-disciplinary care team responsible for clinical issues. A variety of educational, occupational, rehabilitation and social activities are available across a number of off-ward facilities.

Increasing management and staff concern regarding suspicions of illicit drug use amongst patients and related incidents led to the establishment of a working party, in October 1993, to address these issues. Consequently a decision was taken to conduct a survey with a view to obtaining more detailed information than was currently available. Due to the sensitive nature of such an inquiry it was deemed appropriate to investigate staff perceptions of the extent of "the problem". One of the benefits of canvassing staff opinions was the potential for determining the extent of staff knowledge regarding illicit drugs and their use.

Drug misuse and closed institutions

There is a lack of research into drug misuse problems in Special Hospitals. Most of the literature has concentrated on the problems of drug misuse in prisons, the community and local psychiatric hospitals. Wallace (1993) claims that prisons are awash with drugs. He estimates that half of the prison population have substance misuse problems. However, little in the way of co-ordinated treatment is on offer. A national prison survey reports that 41 per cent of prisoners had their first contact with the criminal justice system through the use of drink or drugs. Eighty percent of cases tried in magistrates courts are drink or drug related (HM Prison Service, 1991).

Mathers et al. (1991) found that 34.5 per cent of patients in a psychiatric hospital admitted to using cannabis at least once in their lifetime. 13 per cent of those tested had urine positive for cannabis, with use being more frequent amongst young males. Also, there was a higher likelihood that an initial diagnosis of "psychosis" would be made if patients reported using cannabis or presented a positive urine sample.

Smith (1993) cites US evidence that 47 per cent of schizophrenics and 32 per cent of mood disordered patients living in the community met diagnostic criteria for some form of substance misuse or dependence. Such proportions are considerably greater than for the general population. High rates of drug misuse, or past use, have also been reported amongst young patients, psychiatric inpatient populations, chronic mentally ill living in urban areas, forensic patients and in emergency departments (see Safer, 1987; Toner et al., 1992; Smith et al., 1993; Barbee et al., 1989; Drake, 1989; cited in Smith 1993).

Smith (1993) remarks that much history of substance misuse remains undocumented in clinical notes; hence masking the true extent of the problem. Use of illicit drugs amongst patients with a mental illness in the community is said to be increasing due to a coincidence of deinstitutionalization policy with increasing social acceptance of drugs. Speculative reasons for drug use by chronic mental patients include: downward social drift into areas where drug use is common; attempts to develop a personal identity more acceptable than that of mental patient; to widen social network and build relationships; and self medication of symptoms or side effects of prescribed medication.

It was estimated that in 1990 between ten and twenty thousand people received a custodial sentence as a result of their illegal drug use (Whitehead, 1990). Imprisonment of drug users is a major part of Britain's current drug policy (Tippell, 1989). The system could be improved by making more effective use of non-custodial dispositions available to courts and linking drug users into appropriate agencies.

The Prison Officers' Association (1984) reported that 81 per cent of prison officers perceived there was a serious or very serious problem with drug misuse in prisons. It suggested that the main drugs used were cannabis, heroin and cocaine. They suggested that visitors were the main suppliers of drugs to the prisons along with cultivation of cannabis plants. Prison officers believed that there was some evidence to suggest that acts of violence could be sometimes attributed to misuse of drugs. Training needs of staff were also identified.

Wever (1992) states that present international policy strategies, which concentrate on the reduction of illicit supply of drugs, have failed everywhere in the world. Growing support exists for less confrontative strategies. Such a change in emphasis is part of a reframing of drug related problems as a public health issue (Wodak, 1993).

Hayes (1991) discussed the changing attitudes within the criminal justice system to working with drug misusing offenders. He states that, gradually, the criminal justice system is becoming more positive towards drug users. Recent developments have taken place in prisons, including counselling, advice and education, for those who use drugs and those who are HIV positive. For Hayes, the most appropriate way to improve effectiveness would be to re-orientate staff from an abstinence to a harm reduction model of practice. This is also supported by the Advisory Council on the Misuse of Drugs (1988), with reference to AIDS and drug misuse.

Training needs of prison staff were addressed in research by the Prison Officers Association (1984). 84 per cent of subjects indicated that only a very small number of staff, or none at all, had been trained in the recognition and detection of drugs. It was recognized that very thorough and regular training was needed in this sphere and without such training personal safety of staff as well as the security of the establishment would be jeopardized. It was recommended that staff training should be one of the highest priorities in prison.

Within the prison system Wallace (1993) remarks that much in the way of treatment is offered on an ad hoc basis, with the springing up of a number of separate initiatives around the country. Other input is provided through contact with voluntary bodies, especially in the field of HIV prevention. Such developments have led to small numbers of prison officers becoming trained in dealing with drug misuse problems.

Keene (1993) recommends further development of assessment methods, monitoring and treatment approaches, particularly cognitive-behavioural treatment approaches in prison. Research in the area of treatment for drug misusers has recently focused heavily on such approaches, including harm reduction, relapse prevention, HIV education and awareness as well as attitudes towards drug users (McGregor et al., 1992). The value of abstinence as a measure of success of therapy is questionable. More realistic measures are those of behavioural changes, success being measured by movement towards an increased ability to control drug use (Robertson et al., 1989).

Any treatment inside institutions should usefully include voluntary drug agencies in the community. The voluntary sector can provide supporting networks for prisoners on release. Such liaison requires thought and preparation by both agencies (Ettorre, 1990). Chandler (1993) describes how a young offenders institution worked with external agencies in providing counselling for drug misusers.

There are problems with treatment approaches being carried out in prisons. These might include ensuring privacy and confidentiality. However, in many ways, the prison environment offers the potential for therapeutic intervention. Imprisonment is a reminder of the chaotic lifestyle outside prison and also imposes a routine providing inmates with time to consider the future. It is recommended that time is spent preparing people with drug problems for release in the outside world (Trace, 1988). It is important to establish good relationships with local drugs agencies and to improve services for employment and leisure (Buchanan and Wyke, 1988).

Brochu and Levesque (1990) argue that prisons constitute an ideal structure for preventative work on alcohol/drug misuse. They state that it is important to keep in mind three main requirements: firstly, the importance of evaluating individuals in terms of involvement with the substance, the role of alcohol and drugs in their lifestyle, and willingness and capacity to change. Secondly, the milieu of the prison should be evaluated and, finally, evaluations should be followed by concrete strategies. A clear policy toward drug misuse is needed.

Method

In order to determine the nature and extent of the drug misuse problem at Ashworth Hospital, questionnaires were sent to all patient care team members on each ward in the hospital, and to various off-ward areas responsible for direct patient activity. The response rate was 39.87 per cent.

The questionnaire looked at different aspects of drug misuse in Ashworth Hospital including: the nature of the problems, how the problems are currently handled, perceived staff training needs, therapeutic needs of patients who misuse drugs and ideas for improved management of the problems. The responses were coded and categorized into meaningful and manageable subject areas. The views of Ashworth Hospital Patients' Council were also canvassed.

Results

The returned forms from wards and other areas were analysed and then categorized as follows:

1. Those which had a clearly identified problem; the returns unanimously identifying the existence of perceived drug-related problems. Four wards, three male and one female, and the department responsible for convening patients social functions, were in this category.

2. Those which had a less clearly identified problem; returns either offer contradictory perceptions of extent of problem or state uncertainty. Twelve wards were in this category.

3. Those wards where staff had not identified any problem at all.

The total numbers of patients in Ashworth Hospital perceived to be misusing drugs ranges from 26-67. These figures being the sums of the most conservative and liberal estimates of the numbers involved respectively. Apart from estimates as to the extent of illicit drug use, the survey responses included a wealth of qualitative information which represented staff perceptions of problems, how they are dealt with, training needs and best strategic responses. To make the data more manageable it was decided to organize the response statements into meaningful, specific categories, as follows.

Staff perceptions of drug misuse and related problems

Staff reported that the most common illicit drug used by patients was cannabis. Other substances listed were either reported in the singular, or in a tiny minority, or referred to instances of past problems associated with a particular patient and no longer evident. These included amphetamines, LSD, valium, ecstasy, magic mushrooms and alcohol.

It was reported by staff that illicit drugs caused a general deterioration of mental health, or exacerbation of existing problems. There was reported to be increased aggression and violent behaviour in some patients misusing drugs and sexually disinhibited behaviour directed towards women. It was stated that the ward routine tended to become unsettled, with increased conflict between staff and patients and amongst patients themselves.

Some staff made reference to perceived evidence of a drug-related sub-culture, including visitors being suspected of supplying drugs and parole patients buying and supplying. Patients who didn't want to use drugs were often pressurized into doing so. Such a scenario provides a possible alternate explanation for the reported instances of antisocial behaviour.

Current strategies for managing drug misuse problems

These included a variety of security interventions: urine sampling, room searches, screening parcels on the ward, drug screens, blood tests and loss of parole. Strategies utilized at ward level included; increased observation, seclusion, patients being moved to another ward, confronting patients suspected of drug abuse, banning certain patients from visiting the ward, confiscating drugs, patients wages being cut, discussing issues with the patient care team and stopping visits. Staff felt that their ability to intervene effectively was hampered by the lack of an appropriate hospital policy.

Staff also reported a variety of therapeutic interventions after building up trust with the patient, including; education of the patient and their family about the negative effects of drugs, support, and encouraging patients towards therapeutic groups and/or individual sessions. Staff also stated that they were often frightened to act due to lack of support by management and that the problem should be addressed with visitors who were thought to be bringing drugs into the hospital.

Of the identified current management strategies (Table 1) there is a greater than 2:1 emphasis on security measures, over therapy. No respondents identified staff training as a management strategy. Nearly a third of respondents fail to identify a current strategy. However, most of these respondents are not from the identified problem areas. This may indicate that strategies are reactive rather than proactive.

Respondents were asked to indicate whether or not they were satisfied with current methods of handling perceived problems. Approximately 47 per cent were dissatisfied, with only 12 per cent

Table 1. Current management strategies

Broad category of response	Sum of identified strategies	Percentage of total responses
Security measure	99	48.52
Therapeutic intervention	41	20.09
No current strategy identified	59	28.92
Major problem area	1	0.49
Minor problem area	13	6.37
No problem area	45	22.05

Table 2. Suggested management strategies

Broad category of response	Sum of identified strategies	Percentage of total responses
Therapy	29	7.12
Education	81	19.90
Increase awareness	69	16.95
Policy	27	6.63
Security	148	36.36
General comments	18	4.42
No suggested strategy	35	8.59
Total	407	100

expressing satisfaction. The relatively large numbers of respondents failing to identify current management strategies or suggestions for how to manage drug misuse problems, coupled with the widespread dissatisfaction with how the problem is being managed, may indicate a cogent rationale for staff training.

Suggested improvements to management strategy

Suggested alternatives to current strategies are represented in Table 2, categorized into broad areas of response.

Certain staff thought there was an opportunity to create a specialized unit within Ashworth to deal with illicit drug users. This would involve building up trusting relationships with patients and provision of education and counselling adapted to individual need. It was also thought that providing more constructive activities during the day would help in alleviating boredom, perceived to be a large contributory factor in patients' drug use.

Education and training of staff, patients and visitors, with respect to drug misuse, was considered to be a high priority. Involvement of drug workers and agencies in the community was suggested along with strategies for generally increasing awareness about drug misuse in all areas of the hospital.

Increased security measures were also suggested; controlling the entry of illicit drugs into the hospital, the use of sniffer dogs and detection technology, and prosecution of visitors who are caught bringing drugs in. It was suggested that there should be staff employed specifically to search visitors, due to a conflict in role for nursing staff. Random urine analysis and searching patients were considered useful by some staff. However strip searches were considered unacceptable. It was suggested that certain patients continually abusing illicit drugs could be sent back to prison. Conversely, some staff stated that increased security would exacerbate the problem and there should be a shift of emphasis from one of containment of the problem to a more progressive approach.

Training needs expressed by staff in relation to drug misuse

Staff indicated a number of gaps in knowledge, for which they would like information and education. These ranged from how to deal with the problem as a whole, to requesting information about how other hospitals deal with similar problems. Other education needs revolved around appropriate care planning and the management of patients who are using illicit drugs. Large numbers of respondents were concerned with understanding how to control entry and distribution of drugs into Ashworth and how to control patients access to drugs.

Staff also highlighted concern about their rights under the law with respect to drug use and consequences of use, and where they stood with respect to accountability. Some staff wanted assistance to take a pro-active constructive approach rather than react to the next inevitable problems.

Summary of Patients' Council views

Correspondence from the Council stated that more direct approaches to the drug misuse problem would be difficult and the matter should be handled sensitively. However, they expressed concerns that a serious incident may occur due to factors related to drug misuse.

The Council stated that drug awareness and education of patients should take place. They also suggested that patients' visitors should sensitively be made aware of the problems of bringing in illicit drugs to the hospital. Initially this should be by a discussion with information and advice being made available to the visitor.

Discussion

The perceptions of a drug misuse problem amongst Ashworth patients referred almost exclusively to cannabis. The total number of patients identified as misusing drugs was in the range of 26 to 67. For those staff having to work in the problem areas there are strong feelings of a general lack of support and guidance in how best to address the problem. Explicitly stated was a call for a systematic and co-ordinated policy for dealing with drug related problems. The survey highlighted a wealth of information as to which particular problems staff attributed to drug misuse. Such problems were mainly concerning anti-social behaviour of patients, largely concerned with the supply of illicit substances. Such a view, concentrating on the consequences of illicit drug use, precludes any focus on the reasons why patients are using drugs. These issues would be the demand conditions of any drug use equation and may include problematics of incarceration, boredom, self-esteem, and be related to previous lifestyle.

Staff responses to the survey identify a range of gaps in relevant knowledge indicating a need for co-ordinated education and training in this field. Furthermore, close analysis of some of the response statements would infer the potential for some staff views to be in conflict with a progressive policy. This in itself would indicate the need to structure staff training to deal with both misconceptions about drug use and the promotion of helpful attitudes.

Many of the more serious problems identified as being associated with illicit drug use may be explicable in terms of theories of drug-related sub culture. An important aspect of this is the mechanisms by which individuals construct social roles and maintain status from activities within such a culture. By implication the handling of problems within this system may itself operate in the maintenance of role and status; particularly if patients perceive themselves as being engaged in an ongoing conflict with the representatives of the hospital establishment.

The sociology of sub-culture and deviance is potentially illuminating in this respect (see Cohen, 1955; Taylor et al., 1973). Interestingly, the related concepts of deviancy amplification (Young, 1971) and "moral panic" (Cohen, 1972) could be seen to have pertinence within Ashworth; at the very least being worthy of future investigation. Problems associated with drug use may be exacerbated by heavy handed responses to those labelled "drug misusers". Similarly, a moral panic has been presented in the press coverage of Ashworth's drug problems.

For the staff involved in conducting the survey, and those involved in the many strands of attempting to manage the identified problems, the media circus which has ensued is disquieting and could ultimately prove to exacerbate any drug-related problems in the hospital. The mechanisms by which such a worsening of the situation could occur are complex. However, it is not too simplistic to state that talk of situations of "anarchy" and problems verging on the "epidemic" (Burrell, 1993; Pittam, 1993) could, if we are not careful, turn out to be self-fulfilling prophecy.

This is not to deny the variety of distressing problems which arise for those staff and patients who have to live with the consequences of illicit drug use within a closed institution. Rather, attempts to describe the nature and extent of these problems needs to be undertaken in a realistic and credible manner.

It is acknowledged that certain people at Ashworth have mental health problems which would render them vulnerable to any adverse effects of mind altering substances. However, most of the problems reported in the survey, and (for what it is worth) in the media, do not relate to drug induced episodes of psychosis. It may be more accurate to describe the most pressing problems as arising from the particular culture which develops around drug use within a closed institution. That is to say that the problems experienced by staff and patients within the hospital result more from the activity involved in the supply of drugs, and the maintenance of a counter-culture, than from the direct effects of the drugs themselves. Of course, such a scenario is reflected in the nature of the drug problems exhibited in wider society. Particular problems arise within the closed confines of an institution such as Ashworth, wherein one person's lifestyle is bound to impinge on those of others.

We would suggest that the most harmful consequences of such a scenario need have little to do with the legality of the substance concerned. The solutions, if any can be found, are unlikely to lie in a clampdown on security. If it is accepted that the problems which result for staff and patients who have to live amongst drug taking activity are due mainly to the associated wheeling and dealing, rather than the effects of drugs on individuals, then perhaps the most effective solutions lie in a greater understanding of the conditions which foster such a problem and the implementation of initiatives which seek to remedy them.

Attempts to restrict supply of illicit drugs, in the absence of any other strategy, are almost certainly doomed to failure. This fact has been one of the most clearly demonstrated lessons to be gleaned from previous international research in this area. Hence, the contemporary movement amongst both treatment and drug enforcement agencies toward more progressive policy. Such trends in policy are reflected within the wider penal system and have, most recently, been emphasized in the Woolf Report (1991). The most productive strategies would appear to be those geared towards support and therapy, with attention paid to interventions likely to alleviate or minimize demand conditions.

Conclusions

Within a secure environment there exists a complex set of conditions and human relations, some of which are conducive to maintaining a demand for drugs. Also, many of our patients will not be strangers to illicit drug use prior to admission. Given scepticism regarding the effectiveness of supply orientated policies, it ought to be potentially more useful to seek answers to Ashworth's illicit drug use problems in terms of addressing the demand side of the equation, and attempting to reduce the consequential harm associated with drug use. These twin objectives need not be seen as contradictory (Clements et al., 1990). The challenge for Ashworth staff lies in choosing the most appropriate means by which to pursue effective solutions. The approach needs to be well thought out and sensitively implemented. We suggest that the solutions are to be found in a combination of culture change, attention to the hospital environment and facilities, working with drug using patients therapeutically, providing support for staff, dispelling ignorance, and enabling staff to be proactive through appropriate training. Of course, such an approach ought to be compatible with the stated policy goals of improving the general culture of the hospital, following the public inquiry (Committee of Inquiry, 1992).

It is hoped that an outcome of conducting this survey will be a positive influence on the development of useful management strategies within Ashworth. As such, a number of recommendations have been made, drawing on both information from the survey and the wider literature, and forwarded to the Hospital Management Group. Further research into the alleged sub-cultural aspects of Ashworth's drug misuse problems is planned.

References

ADVISORY COUNCIL ON THE MISUSE OF DRUGS (1988) **Aids and Drug Misuse. Part 1.** London: HMSO

BURRELL, I. (1993) Drugs take jail close to anarchy. **The Sunday Times,** 12 December

BROCHU, S., and LEVESQUE, M. (1990) Treatment of prisoners for alcohol or drug misuse problems. **Alcoholism Treatment Quarterly, 7,** 4, 113-121

BUCHANAN, J., and WYKE, G. (1988) **Drug Specialism in the Probation Service: The first year of the Sefton Drugs Team 1987-8.** Bootle: Sefton Drugs Team

CHANDLER, D. J. (1993) **Report on Drugstop's therapeutic counselling service to H.M. Young Offender Institution Aylesbury for offenders who have been substance dependent.** Aylesbury: Drugstop

CLEMENTS, I., COHEN, J., and KAY, J. (1990) **Taking Drugs Seriously: A manual of harm reduction education on drugs.** Liverpool: Healthwise

COHEN, A. (1955) **Delinquent Boys: The culture of the gang.** Glencoe: Free Press

COHEN, S. (1972) **Folk Devils and Moral Panics.** London: Paladin

COMMITTEE OF INQUIRY (1992) **Report of the Committee of Inquiry into Complaints about Ashworth Hospital. Volume I.** London: HMSO

ETTORRE, B. (1990) The role of the voluntary drug agencies in prison. **Prison Service Journal, 78,** 39-41

HAYES (1991) Changing Goals: The Criminal Justice System and drug misuse. **Justice of the Peace, 155,** 585-587

H. M. PRISON SERVICE (1991) **Caring for Drug Users: A multidisciplinary resource for people working with prisoners.** London: H. M. Prison Service

KEENE, J. (1993) **Drug Use Before and After Prison. A survey of a local prison and probation population in Wales.** Swansea University: Centre for Applied Studies

MATHERS, D. C., GHODSE, A. H., CAAN, A. W., and SCOTT, S. A. (1991) Cannabis use in a large sample of acute psychiatric admissions. **British Journal of Addiction, 86,** 779-784

PITTAM, N. (1993) Hash-worth Hospital. **The Star,** 14 December

ROBERTSON, J. R., BUCKNALL, A. B. V., SKIDMORE, C. A., ROBERTS J. J. K., and SMITH, J. H. (1989) Remission and relapse in heroin users and implications for management: treatment control or risk reduction? **International Journal of Addiction 24,** 3, 229-246

SMITH, J. (1993) Dual diagnosis patients: substance abuse by the severely mentally ill. **British Journal of Hospital Medicine. 50,** 11, 650-654

TAYLOR, I., WALTON, P., and YOUNG, J. (1973) **The New Criminology: For a social theory of deviance.** London: Routledge & Kegan Paul

THE PRISON OFFICERS' ASSOCIATION (1984) **Report into drug abuse in penal establishments in England, Wales and Northern Ireland.** Edmonton: The POA

TIPPELL, S. (1989) Drug users and the prison system. In S. McGregor (Ed.) **Drugs and British Society: Responses to a social problem in the 1980s.** London: Routledge

TRACE, M. (1988) Why not work in prison? **Druglink, 3,** 5, 6-8

WALLACE, J. (1993) Treatment behind bars: a new initiative. **Addiction Counselling World, 4,** 20, 4-7

WEVER, L. (1992) Drug policy changes in Europe and the USA alternatives to international welfare. **International Journal on Drug Policy, 3,** 4, 176-181

WHITEHEAD, G. (1990) Breaking the Dependency. **Social Work Today, 21,** 11 January, 20-21

WODAK, A. (1993) Taming demons: the reduction of harm resulting from use of illicit drugs. **International Journal of Drug Policy, 4,** 2, 72-77

WOOLF, Lord Justice, and TUMIN, S. (1991) **Prison Disturbances. April 1990. Report of an Inquiry by Lord Justice Woolf. Parts 1 and 2.** London: HMSO

YOUNG, J. (1971) **The Drugtakers: The social meaning of drug use.** London: Paladin

An investigation into suicidal behaviours in prison

Polly Dexter and Graham Towl

In this paper we present findings from research which aimed to increase our understanding of the nature and causes of suicidal behaviours in an adult male prison. We give an overview of the findings derived from analyses of record-based and interview-based data. In particular, we discuss the value of a typology of suicidal ideation, and consider the role of environmental, situational and individual factors in the development of suicidal behaviours. We finish by discussing some of the implications for research and practice based on the findings.

In this paper we give a brief review of the literature on suicides in prisons. This is followed by an outline of an empirical study conducted in a prison into suicidal behaviours. The paper ends with a number of recommendations for improved policy and practice in the management of prisoners.

Background

Considerable concern has been expressed in recent years about the incidence of prison suicides. This is largely due to findings which indicate prison suicide rates are considerably higher than rates in the general population.

Much of the research into suicidal behaviours in prison has been descriptive in nature and has aimed to identify individual characteristics associated with these behaviours. The assumption which underlies many of these studies is that there exists a "profile" of the suicidal individual (Liebling, 1992), and that knowledge of the characteristics which define the profile will enable the prediction of those individuals "at risk" of suicide.

Many of the descriptive studies have been criticized on methodological grounds (Lloyd, 1990; Liebling, 1992). However, perhaps their primary weakness is at a theoretical level, namely the dubious assumptions and explanations of behaviour which underlie this research.

In response to the growing evidence that research focusing on individual characteristics was not improving the accuracy of suicide risk assessments in prison, greater emphasis was given to possible environmental and motivational components of prison suicide (e.g. Wool and Dooley, 1987; Dooley, 1990). In addition, the limitations of studies focusing on record-based data led to the development of alternative and more appropriate methodologies. In particular, two extensive studies (Liebling, 1992; Liebling and Krarup, 1993) aimed to develop our understanding of prison suicide by talking to suicidal prisoners to try and understand (the reasons for) their behaviour.

Some of the key findings emerging from the literature

Individual characteristics found to be associated with both community and prison suicides (e.g. poverty, unemployment, educational deprivation, alcohol/drug problems) are also shared by a large proportion of the prison population (e.g. Zamble and Porporino, 1988; Dooley, 1990).

There is not a single profile for prisoner suicide (Liebling, 1992), but there may exist groups of prisoners who are more "at risk" (e.g. the remand population, life sentence prisoners, the mentally ill).

Liebling and Krarup (1993) developed a typology of 7 vulnerable groups of prisoners based on their finding that different aspects of the regime effect prisoners in different ways, partly dependent upon what stage of custody prisoners are at.

Theoretical approaches to suicide and attempted suicide in prison based on the assumption of "psychopathology" are inadequate. Of prison suicides, only approximately one-third have a history of psychiatric in-patient treatment (e.g. Backett, 1987). This is only slightly higher than findings for the general prison population (found to be approximately 22 per cent; Gunn et al., 1978). These models of suicidal behaviours both in prison and in the community do not adequately address the role of social class and environmental factors (e.g. Jack, 1992).

The types of variables most able to distinguish between suicidal prisoners and others, are those relating to the current situation in prison (Liebling, 1992; Liebling and Krarup, 1993). Liebling conceptualizes the cluster of variables found to be associated with vulnerability, within a "coping theory" framework. The argument is that prisoners most "at risk" are those lacking in coping ability.

Research aims

In general terms, this study aimed to:

1. Increase our understanding of the nature of "at risk" behaviours and the causes of suicidal behaviour in prisons, to enable prisoners at significant risk of suicide to be more effectively managed.

2. Empirically investigate the role of environmental factors in suicidal behaviour by examining the incidence of suicidal behaviours in the context of regime changes.

Methodology

The research aims necessitated a two-pronged methodological approach:

1. A record based study.

2. An interview based study.

1. The record based study

Record-based data was used to obtain information on the nature and incidence, (and the response to) suicidal behaviour occuring during the period October 1990 to June 1993. The data was largely derived from the suicide risk referral forms used by prison staff to refer a prisoner, who they suspected presented a significant risk of suicide, to the medical officer for assessment.

2. The interview based study

The interview-based study involved an in-depth investigation of a sample of 22 prisoners defined as "at risk" of suicide during a 6 month period. The operational definition of prisoners "at risk" was:

> prisoners who were distressed, depressed or finding it difficult to cope and experiencing thoughts or feelings of a suicidal nature, and/or prisoners identified as "at risk" by prison staff with a suicide risk referral form.

Data was collected through 3 complementary methods: semi-structured interviews, self-report questionnaires (the Beck Depression Inventory and the Hopelessness Scale), and data from files. The study was longitudinal in design with subjects being interviewed on 3 occasions (i.e. N weeks: N+ 1 week: N+ 4 weeks). Table 1 gives details of "losses" of subjects over time.

Findings

1. Record based study - key findings

a) Incidence of suicidal behaviour in context of regime changes
In September 1991, telephones and new accommodation units were introduced in the prison. The quantitative investigation examined the incidence of records during the period October 1990 to June

Table 1. Details of sample

	1st interview (N weeks)	2nd interview (N + 1 week)	3rd interview (N + 4 weeks)
Declined interview	0	2	1
Unavailable (transferred or discharged)	0	3	2
Number of prisoners interviewed	22	17	14

1993. In the period following September 1991, the number of prisoners identified as at risk of suicide with a suicide risk referral form decreased considerably, and the numbers stabilized at this lower level.

An analysis of the reasons for referral of prisoners at risk of suicide indicated these reasons do not appear to have changed considerably in nature, supporting the idea that it is the incidence of suicidal behaviours which has decreased and not simply decreased reporting.

b) Limitations of recorded information
This study highlighted difficulties relating to the use of record-based data in research into suicidal behaviours in prisons. Some of the records were incomplete. For example, in 16 per cent of cases there was no recorded medical assessment. There was also evidence of inconsistencies in the type of information provided, and indications that records were being "lost".

2. Interview based study - key findings

a) Nature of suicidal behaviour
There was evidence for some degree of "suicidal behaviour" in all 22 prisoners interviewed, ranging from thoughts indirectly related to suicide to attempts at suicide. Four prisoners had self-injured (defined where a prisoner stated he had injured himself but had no intention of killing himself) and a further 2 prisoners had attempted suicide (defined where a prisoner had injured himself and stated he had intended to kill himself). A typology of suicidal ideation was developed in line with four different "types" of suicidal thoughts which emerged from prisoners' reports of their thoughts.

An ideational typology:

a. Thoughts indirectly related to suicide, but no evidence of their having considered suicide as a possible or desired option.

b. Thoughts suggesting they have considered committing suicide, but have no intention of carrying it out.

c. Thoughts suggesting they would like to commit suicide, but no evidence of them having made plans to carry it out.

d. Thoughts indicating they would like to commit suicide and they have planned how to do it.

These four ideational types, or styles, may be helpful in aiding clinical decision-making. A score of 9 or above on the Hopelessness Scale has been found to indicate suicide intent (Beck et al., 1975). The mean Hopelessness Scale scores for prisoners whose thoughts were grouped into categories a and b, were under the cut-off score of 9. In contrast, the mean Hopelessness Scale scores for prisoners whose suicidal thoughts were classified into categories c and d, ranged from 12 to 15, indicating these prisoners were more "at risk" of committing suicide.

Prisoners who had self-injured were not necessarily more at risk of suicide than those who had not. Importantly, this suggests that a consideration of an individual's thoughts and feelings may facilitate a more comprehensive assessment of suicide risk in incidents of self-injury.

b) Factors contributing to suicidal behaviour
The majority of prisoners reported various reasons for their current difficulties. In all 22 cases, details of the immediate antecedents which appeared to trigger the crisis and the prisoners' primary reason for the crisis was gathered during interview, and grouped into categories (relationship/famiiy problems; prison pressures/system frustrations; discharge worries; psychological problems).

A breakdown of the number of prisoners reporting difficulties within each of the problem categories was undertaken, in terms of the immediate antecedent and the major problem given for their crisis.

A large proportion of the sample reported difficulties within different problem categories. For many, various problems had contributed to their current distress. In some cases, the immediate antecedent was reported to be the primary reason for the crisis. For others, the immediate antecedent was a trigger at a time when they were struggling to deal with other difficulties.

Frequently, there were various individual, situational and environmental factors, which although not initially identified as causes by the prisoner, could be seen through interview to have contributed to their distress/crisis.

i) Individual factors

Background information: a significant proportion of the 22 prisoners interviewed had experienced an emotionally deprived childhood. Six prisoners described suffering sexual and/or physical abuse, a further 5 felt they were neglected emotionally. The majority of prisoners had poor educational and employment histories. Seventeen (77 per cent) were unemployed prior to arrest for their present conviction. Half of the sample reported regularly misusing drugs or alcohol prior to their imprisonment. There was evidence of formal psychiatric contact in 7 prisoners' backgrounds prior to their current sentence (ranging from visits from a psychiatric nurse to in-patient psychiatric care). Seven prisoners had previously attempted suicide and subsequently been admitted to hospital. A further 3 reported previously injuring themselves, but had not reported their injuries.

Current characteristics

Depression and hopelessness: all prisoners were suffering from at least some of the symptoms of depression. Table 2 provides the Beck Depression Inventory (BDI) scores for the prisoners interviewed at the 3 interview stages. Table 3 shows the Hopelessness Scale scores for prisoners interviewed: a score of 9 or above has been found to indicate suicide intent (Beck et al., 1974).

Table 2. Beck Depression Inventory (BDI) scores

| | Number of prisoners at each interview stage scoring* | | | | | |
	0-9	10-18	19-25	26-35	36 and over	Mean average score
First interview	0	8	8	4	2	21.6
Second interview	0	2	10	3	2	23.9
Third interview	1	3	3	3	0	21.1

* where score ranges indicate (Beck et al., 1961):

0-9	"normal"
10-18	mild depression
19-25	moderate depression
26-35	moderate to severe depression
36 and above	severe depression

Table 3. Hopelessness Scale scores

| | Number of prisoners at each interview stage scoring | | |
	8 or below	9 or above	Mean average score
First interview	7	15	10.5
Second interview	5	12	10.1
Third interview	4	6	8.7

Coping skills: information on coping strategies used by prisoners inside and outside of prison was collected. The coping strategies prisoners employed were categorized according to their function (based on a set devised by Zamble and Porporino, 1987). The categories were as follows:

1. None - no strategy employed to attempt to cope with the situation.

2. Reactive problem-solving - attempts are made to cope with the situation, but they lack evidence of persistence, planning or consideration of consequences.

3. Avoidance or escape - from the situation or from thoughts about it.

4. Palliative - including responses made to reduce the emotional distress caused by the problem situation, often by providing some contrasting pleasant experience.

5. Social support - use of others for comfort, support, reassurance or sharing of problems.

6. Cognitive reinterpretive strategies - use of cognitive techniques to alter their emotional response to their situation, or changes in their appraisal or perception of the situation to reduce the perceived threat.

7. Anticipatory substitution - deliberate choice of behaviours incompatible with occurrence of problem situation, generally using strategy of filling time.

8. Anticipatory problem-oriented - explicit recognition of nature of problem situation: systematic, organized and persistent attempts to resolve the situation and evidence of planning and anticipation of future results.

Table 4 gives details of the number of prisoners indicating they used each of the strategies outside and inside prison.

Table 4. Coping strategies used inside and outside prison

Category	Number of sample using	
	Outside prison	Inside prison
1. None	3	12
2. Reactive problem-solving	17	18
3. Avoidance or escape	14	18
4. Palliative	14	5
5. Social support	13	5
6. Cognitive reinterpretative	2	7
7. Anticipatory substitution	1	7
8. Anticipatory problem-oriented	5	3

Reactive problem-solving and avoidance or escape were the strategies most commonly used both inside and outside prison. The number of prisoners using anticipatory substitution, cognitive re-interpretive strategies and feeling "they could do nothing at all", all increased in prison. Importantly, prisoners had often tried to avoid their problems or had used reactive problem solving and in some cases used anticipatory problem solving. The failure of their attempts to improve the situation appeared to have triggered them to "give up".

ii) Situational factors

Although the difficulties prisoners were experiencing in relation to their situation varied, certain themes were evident. In particular:

Difficulties in relationships with people outside prison: thirteen of the interviewed prisoners reported relationship difficulties to be contributing or to have caused their current distress (e.g. by evoking feelings of failure, resentment, guilt or anger, at the relationship having failed; in feelings of hopelessness with regard to the future; in concerns about the welfare of children or disatisfaction with access arrangements).

Future prospects: a number of the prisoners described perceiving their future prospects to be poor. Some had nowhere to live, few or no friends or family, no employment and felt there was nothing available to help them with their problems (e.g. drink/drug problems). For some prisoners, it seemed to be the hopelessness of the future which was to a large extent causing their distress, or exacerbating their current difficulties and inhibiting their ability to cope.

iii) The prison environment

The majority of prisoners reported that aspects of the prison environment exacerbated or contributed to their current difficulties or distress. The prison management response to prisoners who expressed their distress was frequently limited to the segregation of the prisoner (sometimes in strip conditions). This usually increased feelings of hopelessness.

Two prisoners who were located in the segregation unit described how their difficulties were largely created by their location. Their forced inactivity, lack of contact with other prisoners or staff, meant they frequently spent long periods ruminating about their problems and the hopelessness of their situation. Clearly, segregation is not an apropriate strategy for dealing with vulnerable prisoners, as often it can exacerbate rather than ameliorate their difficulties.

As well as the formal response, the informal response by prison staff to "at risk" prisoners can be a significant factor in prisoner suicidal behaviours. An uncaring comment by a member of staff may, in effect, be "the last straw". Staff attitudes and associated levels of professionalism vary considerably, and may work against a positive approach to suicide awareness and prevention. There were indications that some staff (both hospital and discipline officers) show a reluctance to help vulnerable prisoners, believing it is not their responsibility, or even that these prisoners are not deserving of their help.

c) The Managaement and care of prisoners at risk of suicide

i) Identifying prisoners "at risk" of suicide

There was considerable evidence that during the study period several "at risk" prisoners (including 3 who had self-injured) had not been identified as such with a suicide risk referral form. Although these prisoners had been referred by staff who considered that they "appeared depressed or possibly suicidal or who they considered were finding it difficult to cope", there was no evidence to suggest these prisoners were receiving any help or support.

ii) Assessment of prisoners identified as at risk of suicide with a suicide risk referral form

Where prisoners had been identified as "at risk" with a referral form, policy guidelines state that a medical assessment should be undertaken. The record-based study found that in 16 per cent of cases there was no recorded medical assessment. In the majority of cases (38 of 69), the medical assessment found the prisoner identified as "at risk" to be "not suicidal at present". Sixteen of the assessments concluded "not a risk", "no-risk" and "not suicidal". In 22 assessments, statements were qualified with, for example, "not suicidal at present" or "he says he's not feeling suicidal". There was evidence in several assessments of negative motives being attributed to the prisoner's behaviour (e.g. "this inmate is manipulative", "this incident is attention seeking"). Few assessments detailed the reasons or problems underlying the prisoners difficulties.

iii) Response to prisoners identified as "at risk"

The record-based study involved an analysis of the medical instructions stated on the 69 suicide risk referral forms (between October 1990 and June 1993).

The most common instructions stated on the referral forms were "general observation", "segregation and 15 minute observations", and "referral of the prisoner to other members of staff" (e.g. probation, psychology, chaplain). There was no follow up information provided on the forms about further assessments during, for example, the period of segregation or on whether or not the prisoner was actually seen by other members of staff.

Four of the five prisoners interviewed in the study, who were segregated and observed every 15 minutes, reported that this experience had increased their feelings of distress and despair. There was evidence that for some prisoners (including those not formally identified as a suicide risk), the experience or fear of segregation encouraged them to deny any suicidal thoughts. Another belief or fear held by some prisoners was that if they expressed their feelings, they would be transferred to a prison hospital, an outcome most of them wished to avoid.

Some methodological limitations

The study found some evidence that the number of suicide risk referral forms decreased with the implementation of new accommodation and telephones. Interpretations of this finding must be cautious. The investigation into the incidence of referral forms before and after regime changes employed record-based data, the limitations of which are well documented (e.g. Liebling, 1992). The retrospective nature of this aspect of the study meant other variables whch may have contributed to the decrease in referral forms were often not available for analysis or not quantifiable (e.g. staff morale, growth of personal officer scheme, relationships between staff and prisoners). In addition, since the telephones and the new accommodation were implemented over the same period, it was not possible to assess the independent contribution of each of these to the decrease in the rate of suicide risk referral forms.

The small scale of the interview-based study and its focus on "at risk" prisoners in a single prison, limit the generalizability of the findings.

Conclusions

a) Nature of suicidal behaviour

This study proposes a typology of suicidal ideation which may be helpful in distinguishing behaviours which are more, and those which are less, closely related to suicide. This typology is consistent with a conceptualization of suicidal behaviour as a continuum, along which some individuals may move, and others may not. The typology of suicidal thoughts differentiate between prisoners who are clearly distressed but not necessarily suicidal, and those whose distress is accompanied by despair and who represent a higher risk of suicide.

This typology of suicidal ideation has implications for both research (e.g. in distinguishing suicidal behaviours) and clinical practice (e.g. in addressing the level of risk of suicide).

b) Understanding suicidal behaviours in prison

To understand the development of suicidal behaviours within the prison environment, it is necessary to consider the interaction of factors relating to the individual, his background and his present situation (including the prison environment he is in, and his circumstances outside). Features within the individual's history may be helpful in understanding his or her vulnerability but generally do not distinguish prisoners at risk of suicide, i.e. a large proportion of the general prison population have come from unstable backgrounds, have poor educational and employment histories and have misused alcohol/drugs. Some of these factors contributed to the prisoners' reported hopelessness about their future upon release (e.g. few stable relationships, nowhere to live and unemployment).

Frequently, prisoners perceived problems which they were having difficulties managing or solving to have caused their distress. The most common problems related to relationship or family concerns and often linked to this, discharge concerns. Many prisoners, but significantly not all prisoners, appeared not to possess effective coping skills. There was evidence that some prisoners had made systematic efforts to analyse their problems and considered various ways of dealing with them. For these prisoners, it appeared to be the repeated failure of their attempts to alter the situation which triggered them to "give up". This indicates that, as Beck (1975) suggests, the hopelessness may inhibit coping in these prisoners, by reducing expectations of any improvement in their situation. The central issue which needs addressing is what triggers the hopelessness or negative expectations. There was some indication that prisoners' perceptions of their ability to control aspects of their life could help us to understand the role of the prison environment in the development of hopelessness. For the majority of prisoners, there were indications that they generally perceived their lifestyle, problems and future to be outside their control. However, for those who possessed the coping skills, the experience of feeling their problems were out of their control appeared to be more particular to their current situation and the prison environment. The importance of perceptions has been explored by Jack (1992) in relation to women who attempt suicide. He argues that some women acquire, through their socialization, a "helpless" attributional style - they perceive their problems to be outside their control - which renders them less able to cope. When their problems are not solved, the helplessness may turn to hopelessness, and suicide may become a desired option. It is possible this theory may be applied to suicidal behaviour in prisoners, as it enables an appreciation of the interaction between social factors, psychological factors characterizing prisoners "at risk" (e.g. their hopelessness and expressed helplessness), and the prison environment, which can exacerbate difficulties by taking away more control from the individual.

c) Managing and caring for prisoners "at risk"

This study found evidence that our increased understanding of suicidal behaviours is not matched by improvements in the care of vulnerable prisoners. Segregation of prisoners, often in "strip" conditions, continues to be a formally legitimated humiliation ritual which distressed prisoners must sometimes endure. Clearly, this response is not acceptable; such conditions are inhumane and punish prisoners for their distress, exacerbating feelings of despair and encouraging prisoners to deny their suicidal feelings. In addition, there were indications that some staff, on an informal basis, may be instrumental in creating a punitive response to vulnerable prisoners.

This study has shown that "risk" can fluctuate over time partly contingent upon the individual's perception of his situation. Assessments of risk as currently included in prison documentation are in many cases conceptually unsound, e.g. by viewing "risk" as a dichotomous variable. The attribution of "manipulative" motives to suicidal behaviour, evident in the medical assessments, are dangerous. They effectively label the behaviour as not worthy of care and support and encourage the adoption of unsympathetic and hostile attitudes, which may drive "at risk" prisoners to suicide.

The study found tentative evidence to support the positive role of general improvements (e.g. access to telephones) in the prison environment in suicide prevention strategies.

Recommendations

A broad range of measures are required to enable prisoners to more effectively cope with imprisonment. We may usefully conceptualize prison regimes as constituting 3 sets of resources - staff, prisoners and facilities. Our recommendations are structured to focus upon maximizing best practice in the use of these sets of resources and minimizing poor practices.

1. Staff

i) Recruitment

Part of the recruitment method should include an exercise where prospective staff have the opportunity to demonstrate skills in helping a "prisoner" experiencing coping difficulties. Also, at a more general level, the candidates "attitude to prisoners" should be formally assessed.

ii) Training

In general terms, we would endorse the main thrust of the current suicide awareness package which requires widespread dissemination. Residential unit prison officer management grades, i.e. senior officers and principal officers, should ideally be responsible for the package delivery. It is important that the training is evaluated.

iii) Management

Managers in prisons have a general responsibility to ensure that language used by staff is not offensive and/or damaging to groups or individuals. In the suicide awareness training package, "staff sayings" about suicide, from previous research, are included, e.g. "I'll give you a new razor blade so that you can slash your wrists". Such sayings in the package are accounted for in terms of being "not representative of the opinions and values held by staff, and are sometimes motivated by defensiveness or stress, it is clear that this kind of language can give a bad impression to prisoners, visitors and colleagues". This, simply, is not good enough. What should be included in the training package at this juncture is a clear statement that staff making such comments, i) could trigger another death in custody, and ii) would be subject to disciplinary proceedings. Also, other terms such as "manipulative" and "attention seeking" are sometimes used to dangerous and destructive effect. We recommend that managers are empowered to take disciplinary action against staff for such degrading linguistic practices.

2. Prisoners

i) Listener scheme

There remains a great deal of scope for the further development of "listener schemes" in prisons. In some prisons, these schemes have been extended to enable "listeners" to provide close or even continuous supervision in an appropriate environment for prisoners assessed to be suicidal. We would endorse this positive move towards a more constructive response to distressed prisoners.

Prisoners should be encouraged to have an active involvement in the development of suicide and self-injury prevention procedures within prisons (e.g. representatives attending suicide awareness group meetings, vulnerable prisoners attending their own case conferences).

3. Facilities

* Ensure that prisoners have access to "positive regimes", e.g. the opportunity to participate in constructive supervised activities, good accommodation, telephones and appropriate visiting opportunities.

* Ensure a flexible response to the needs of prisoners especially at times when they are identified as at highest risk of suicide, e.g. assistance could be provided in structuring the days activities.

* Strip cell conditions should not be used. There needs to be a shift in emphasis from the physical prevention of suicides (by removal of all potential suicide implements) to the provision of care and support from other prisoners or staff to encourage and help vulnerable prisoners find alternative solutions to their problems

* Ensure that prisoners, if suicidal, are not sent to "segregation units" for "punishment", but rather to specialist facilities (e.g. "care rooms") developed within the prison for care and support.

Above, we have outlined a number of recommendations which we hope will be of help in informing the more effective management of potentially suicidal prisoners.

References

BACKETT, S. (1987) Suicides in Scottish prisons. **British Journal of Psychiatry, 151**, 218-221

BACKETT, S. (1988) Suicide and Stress in Prison. In S. Backett, J. McNeil and A. Yellowlees (Eds) **Imprisonment Today.** London: Macmillan

BECK, A. T., WEISSMAN, A., LESTER, D., and TREXIER, L. (1974) The measurement of pessimism: the Hopelessness Scale. **Journal of Consulting and Clinical Psycholooy, 42**, 861-865

BECK, A. T., KOVACS, M., and WEISSMAN, A. (1975) Hopelessness and suicidal behaviour. **Journal of the American Medical Association, 234**, 11, 1146-1149

DOOLEY, E. (1990) Prison suicide in England and Wales 1972-1987. **British Journal of Psychiatry, 156**, 40-45

FARRINGTON, D. P. (1978) The family backgrounds of aggressive youths. In L. Hersov and M. Berger (Eds) **Aggression and Anti-social Behaviour in Children and Adolescents.** Oxford: Pergamon Press

GUNN, J., ROBERTSON, G., DELL, S., and WAY, C. (1978) **Psychiatric Aspects of Imprisonment.** London: Academic Press

JACK, R. (1992) **Women and Attempted Suicide.** Hove: Lawrence Erlbaum Associates

LAZARUS, R. S. (1966) **Psychological Stress and the Coping Process.** New York: McGraw Hill

LIEBLING, A. (1992) **Suicide in Prison.** London: Routledge

LIEBLING, A., and KRARUP, H. (1993) **Suicide Attempts in Male Prisons.** Report submitted to Home Office, Institute of Criminology: Cambridge

LLOYD, C. (1990) **Suicide in Prison: A Literature Review.** Home Office Research Study 115. London: HORPU

PORPORINO, F. J., and ZAMBLE, E. (1984) Coping with Imprisonment. **Canadian Journal of Criminology, 26**, 403-421

Bullying among young offenders in custody

Graham Beck

"Bullying" is a generic term which desribes a broad range of anti-social, violent, threatening, domineering and acquisitive behaviours. Usually it refers to persistent aggressive behaviours designed and intended to cause distress and fear over a period of time. In prisons it is used to refer to a wide variety of acts of delinquency within the institutional setting. This paper discusses the prevalence and frequency of bullying among young offenders in prison, some of the behaviours that are recorded and some ways that prisons have responded. It is argued that the bullying which occurs in prison is closely related to the behaviours that led to imprisonment for many offenders. As such, managing bullying is closely related to the modifying of offending behaviour and faces similar challenges.

"Bullying" is a generic term which describes a broad range of antisocial, violent, threatening, domineering and acquisitive behaviours. Usually it refers to "persistent aggressive behaviours, designed and intended to cause distress and fear over a period of time" (Tattum and Herbert, 1990). Definitions have varied to some degree but Farrington (1994) suggests that the main elements are:

1. Verbal, physical or psychological attack or intimidation;

2. Intended to, and does cause fear, distress and harm to the victim;

3. Involving an imbalance of power;

4. Unprovoked by the victim;

5. Repeated over a long time period.

(Farrington, 1994).

In prisons, the term is used to refer to a wide variety of acts of delinquency within the institutional setting, many of which come to be discussed in colloquial terms. For example, prisoners may extort articles such as tobacco or radios from others using threats of violence. This has come to be referred to in many instances as "taxing" and in some cases "baroning" where a dominant individual or group appear to "control" the movement of goods in a communal area. Issues about the definition of bullying in prisons will be discussed in more detail later.

If we consider the population of young offender institutions it might be argued that the past behaviour of prisoners, i.e., that for which they are convicted is consistent with bullying. In this graph offences are classified in four bands:

* *violence against the person* includes murder, attempted murder, manslaughter, wounding, assaults, possession of firearms with intent;

* *acquisitive* offences include burglary, theft, TADA, robbery and receiving stolen goods;

* *sex* offences include rape, indecent assault etc.; and

* *other* includes fraud, forgery, criminal damage, drugs offences, arson, driving offences, breaches of bail or other conditions etc.

With over half of this population being convicted of offences involving theft, and a further 18.8 per cent being convicted for violent crimes, it may be of no surprise that theft and violence occur between prisoners. The labelling of theft and violence in prison as "bullying" may do little more than obscure the observation of consistency of behaviour. The view that bullying and delinquency are linked is supported by evidence from research conducted by Olweus in Norway, who found that those people who had bullied others at school were four times as likely as non-bullies to have three or more convictions later in life (Olweus, 1989; Smith, 1991).

Added to the factor of past behaviour, are the realities and perceptions of prison life. Resources that may be taken for granted as freely available outside prison, become highly valued "inside". Tobacco, sweets and telephone cards are expensive in relation to prisoners' pay, and as such are the focus of intense competition. Added to this are the demands of a new routine when entering prison. In YOIs the movement of people is often so frequent that new prisoners will arrive on most days of the year, particularly where the prison holds remand prisoners. New prisoners will be expected to fit in with the demands of the institution quickly as well as responding to the demands of other prisoners.

The circumstances of imprisonment may be argued to be "ideal" conditions for bullying to occur. Bullying is reported to occur in virtually any form of social institution (although the research literature has focused mainly on childhood and the school environment), and the demanding aspects of the prison environment, allied with the past behaviour of their prisoners, provide a combination where frequent bullying should be expected.

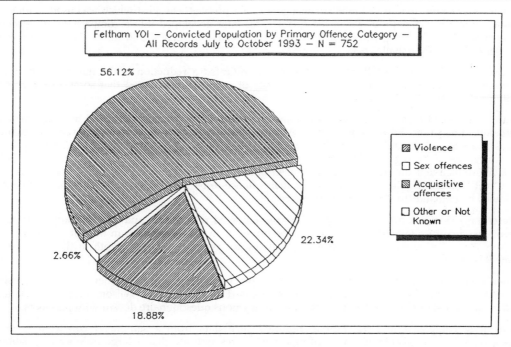

Figure 1. Breakdown of current offences in a sample of convicted young offenders

Previous research in prisons

At this stage it seems appropriate to turn to previous research conducted within the penal setting.

The first published research into bullying in a British prison was that conducted by McGurk and McDougall (1979). The study reports the findings of interviews with 23 prisoners living in a borstal in the north of England. The borstal housed its "trainees" in dormitories, 18 to each dormitory, and the research was solicited by the Governor. McGurk and McDougall describe the dormitories as "unsupervised (and unsupervisable) at night" and go on to note that the previous 100 recorded disciplinary offences reveal only one case of bullying, suggesting that detection and apprehension is highly unlikely (McGurk and McDougall, 1986, 1991, 1993). They state "... the conditions for bullying to occur exist par excellence". Fourteen of the 23 prisoners interviewed said they had witnessed bullying at least once in the last week.

This paper goes on to provide descriptions of the nature of bullying at that time. These descriptions include the following (paraphrased from their research):

1. A *Tetley* - a trainee, naked except for a pair of underpants on his head, with a broom in his hand sings a song ... and dances round the dormitory. Sometimes the inmate is tied to the bed and the broomstick is pushed into his rectum.

2. A *Kestrel* - a cup of water is placed on the pillow of a sleeping inmate and a boot is thrown at him ...

3. An *Eagle* - similar to a *Kestrel* but involving a fire bucket on the bedside table.

4. A *Whodunit* - a blanket is thrown over a trainee and he is beaten or kicked.

5. *Dormitory Death Runs* - an initiation ceremony in which a new trainee has to run down a corridor of trainees who hot them with pillowcases, some of which contain boots.

Other examples included assaults, sexual assaults, enforced drinking of urine and forcing a prisoner to complete tasks for another prisoner as his servant (known as a *Joey*).

McDougall and McGurk presented a range of preventative measures which included enhancing the observation of dormitories, reducing boredom by providing TVs, selecting trainees to live in dormitories according to their past behaviour, training staff, increasing penalties for bullying offences and improving induction facilities.

This final recommendation included the instigation of a problem checklist which was used to identify people who may suffer problems in the prison. This later developed into a comprehensive selection procedure which divides prisoners into categories of behaviour "types" and mixes them according to pre-defined rules (Marshall, 1993).

McGurk and McDougall's follow-up in this study indicated a reduction in the number of bullying incidents reported and also a reduction in severity of events. It was noted that some new forms of bullying also appeared during the period of the study.

In an unpublished report in another YOI, Shine and Wilson (1988) report that most bullying involves initiation into a unit. From their interviews with prisoners and staff, this was thought to mainly involve taunts and threats, occasionally escalating to acts of violence. They divided other behaviours into categories of "taxing" and "baroning" which are thought to occur at other stages of sentence. Such behaviours included the demanding of canteen goods as "protection", sex offenders being forced to "pay" with goods in order for the nature of their offence to be kept secret, and the loaning of goods, followed by demands for "payment with interest".

Interestingly, McGurk and McDougall do discuss enforced repayments and theft but appear to have uncovered a culture involving bullying "for the fun of it" in the dormitories in their study. Shine and Wilson (1988) had moved on to discussing bullying for property in more depth in the YOI system some 9 years later.

Other studies in prisons have sought to assess the prevalence and frequency of bullying using quantitative methods rather then interviews as used by Shine and Wilson, and McGurk and McDougall. Most of these studies have used an anonymous questionnaire design with prisoners.

In a study completed in 1992, Bunton reported such data from a sample of convicted juvenile offenders (14- to 17-years-old). Her self-report measures indicate that a large number of prisoners reported being "tested out" on arrival in their living unit (44 per cent in her sample).

* 39 per cent reported only feeling safe when locked in their cells;

* 83 per cent reported knowing of people stealing personal property; and

* 50 per cent reporting intimidation by other prisoners.

These findings reveal that, among this group, bullying could be argued to be the norm rather than the exception, and that the experience of being intimidated when first arriving in the YOI is part of the experience of imprisonment.

These figures were supported by findings from the Directorate of Programmes (DIP) Research and Regimes Development Group (RRD) which showed that from a national sample of 538 young men in YOIs in 1989, 47 per cent reported some victimization in responses on a Custodial Adjustment Questionnaire. Interesting differences were found between means for groups, such as the higher victimization scores of 17- to 18-year-olds compared to 19- to 21-year-olds (p<.001), sex and arson current offenders scored higher than other offence groups and a relationship between victimization and reporting to "dislike PE".

The author of a summary of this research (DIP, unpublished) notes that there was no relationship between time served and reported victimization. She states:

> this is rather surprising; one would expect that the longer the inmate has been inside, the more opportunity there would have been for these things to happen to him. It suggests that if an inmate is going to be bullied, it will happen fairly quickly (DIP, 1989).

The author also notes that the relationship between self-injury and reported victimization is complex. Those who had self-injured prior to arrival at their current prison scored higher than those having never self-injured, but lower than those who had self-injured in their current YOI. This suggests that self-injury might predate bullying and be a response to it.

Table 1. Prisoners' reported ages

Age	Number	%
15	2	0.6
16	7	2.3
17	51	16.5
18	73	23.5
19	70	22.6
20	102	32.9
21	5	1.6
(3 did not answer)		

Table 2. The ethnic origins of the subjects

Ethnic origin	N	%
White	244	78.0
Black Caribbean	12	3.8
Black African	3	1.0
Asian	9	2.9
Other	5	1.6
Missing	40	12.8

Table 3. Legal status

Legal status	N	%
Remanded	123	39.3
On trial	28	8.9
Convicted awaiting sentence	58	18.5
Convicted and sentenced	101	32.3

The current research

The survey reported in this paper was conducted in two YOIs in late 1993 and early 1994. The intention was to provide some information about the prevalence of bullying, the types of bullying being reported and locations where it was occurring. Both institutions have active anti-bullying groups comprising a multi-disciplinary team who devise strategies to limit the extent of bullying within their prisons, and the surveys were designed to aid the development of strategies and provide a base-line measure against which change could be assessed.

Questionnaires were completed by 313 prisoners in two young offender institutions (YOIs) in November 1993 and February 1994 (referred to here as Prison A and Prison B). The two prisons house around 600 prisoners who are remanded in custody, on trial, convicted but unsentenced or convicted and sentenced.

Population characteristics

120 subjects (38.3 per cent) reported to be in prison for the first time. It is not necessarily clear that all of these prisoners will be entirely new to the particular establishment as some may have been transferred to these two prisons following stays elsewhere and may have responded "yes" as this is their first period in prison custody. However, a recent survey of all arriving prisoners in one month using information from files, showed that 34.8 per cent had no history of prior imprisonment, corroborating this result.

In terms of the length of time subjects had been in their current prison, the reported figures can only be regarded as estimates as the questionnaires were adapted in the second sample to simplify this question. 50 per cent of the sample reported to have been in their prison for 8 weeks or less.

The questionnaire

The questionnaire comprises 12 questions about prisoners' backgrounds and their impressions of the prison, and 16 questions relating to bullying. The questionnaire was adapted from a questionnaire

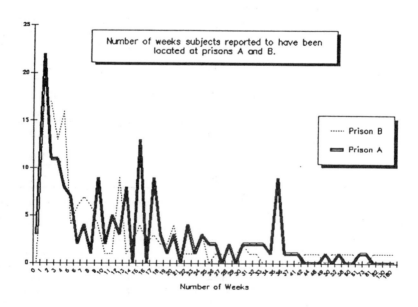

Figure 2. Number of weeks subjects reported to have been located at prisons A and B

designed by Olweus (1989) and adapted by Smith (1991) for use in English schools. A definition of bullying was included on the questionnaire as:

> We say it is bullying when someone deliberately hurts, threatens or frightens someone either in order to take things from them or just for the fun of it.

Method

Questionnaires were distributed to prisoners either in their cells during a "lock-up" period, or handed to them when they collected their meals. They were informed that the survey was designed to help provide information about events in the prison and that all responses were regarded as anonymous. The subjects were instructed not to identify themselves on the form.

The administration was conducted by either a psychologist, a psychological assistant or a probation officer. The first survey was administered over two consecutive days in November 1993, the second was completed on one day in February 1994. The first survey was administered to 50 per cent of the population on the two days of the survey, and subjects were selected using alternate cell numbers. The second survey aimed to include all prisoners in the institution on the day of the survey. Both prisons produce people for court appearances and transfer prisoners throughout the day so the population is not stable, even over a short time period.

The questionnaires were collected at normal unlock time (between 20 minutes and an hour after being given the questionnaire).

Results

A total of 374 questionnaires were handed out and 313 were returned complete (83.7 per cent), 164 from Prison A and 149 from Prison B.

66 prisoners reported to have been bullied in their current prison (21.1 per cent) and 16 prisoners (5.1 per cent) did not answer this question. The proportion of prisoners reporting to be bullied was higher at Prison B (25.2 per cent) than Prison A (19.6 per cent) but the association was not statistically significant ($X^2 = 1.32$; p>.2).

25 prisoners reported to have bullied others (8 per cent of the whole population) and 25 did not answer this question. That is 263 prisoners (84 per cent) of the sample reported that they had not bullied anyone in their current prison. Prison B had a higher proportion of reported bullies (10.5 per cent) as compared to Prison A (7.1 per cent), but the association between bullying and location was again not significant ($X^2 = 1.06$; p>.3).

10 prisoners reported to have both bullied and been bullied; 3.6 per cent of all subjects who answered both questions. This represents 40 per cent of those who report to have bullied and 15.9 per cent of the people who report to have been bullied. This number is high enough to yield a statistically significant association between reporting to be bullied and reporting to have bullied ($X^2 = 4.77$; p< .05).

The orders varied for the two prisons but "threatened" was highest in both. Prison B had "belongings taken" as the next highest which was fifth most common at Prison A. The five most common items were the same in each prison.

The order of locations was different in the two prisons. In Prison B, which has a design of reception unit in which it is difficult to supervise prisoners, this area was the most common location for bullying, but was least common at Prison A. The next four locations were all common locations: association, meal times, canteen (where prisoners collect goods from a central prison shop), and after lock-up at night.

Again the order was different for the two prisons, with Prison A subjects reporting "belongings taken/taxed" and "hit/kicked" as the most common methods, followed by "threat", "racial name calling", "other name calling", and "saying things about someone that were untrue". Prison A subjects reported "threats" as most common followed by "calling names", "belongings taken/taxed" and "hit/kicked".

Locations varied as before, with "reception" being rated as the most common location in Prison B, followed by "association", "canteen", "meal times", "after lock-up", "gym", "education", "between the unit and elsewhere" and "exercise". At prison A the most common area was "association" followed by "exercise", "reception", "gym", "canteen", "meal times", "between the unit and elsewhere" and "after lock-up".

Table 4. Types of bullying reported by "victims"

Rank	Type of bullying	N
1	Threatened	39
2	Called names	35
3	Belongings taken or "taxed"	32
4=	Hit or kicked	31
4=	People saying things about you that are untrue	31
6	Being asked to bring drugs into the priscn	12
7	Called names about my colour	8
8	No one would talk to me	7
9	Other	6

Table 5. The locations where bullying was reported

Rank	Location	N
1	On association	33
2	In reception	26
3	After lock-up at night	24
4	On your way to or from canteen	23
5	Meal times	20
6	Between your unit and somewhere else	18
7	Between the unit and visits	13
8	Exercise	11
9=	In the gym	10
9=	Somewhere else	10
11	At education	9

Table 6. The types of bullying reported by those who said they had bullied others

Rank	Location	N
1	Threatened	18
2=	Hit or kicked	17
2=	Taken belongings/taxed	17
4	Called names	13
5=	Called names about their colour	8
5=	Saying things about them that are untrue	8
7=	Not talking to them	7
	Other	7
	Asking to bring drugs in	5

Table 7. Locations reported

Rank	Location	N
1	Association	16
2	Reception	14
3	On way back from canteen	11
4=	Exercise	10
4=	Meal times	10
4=	Gym	10
7=	After lock-up	9
7=	Between the unit and somewhere else	9
7=	Education	9
10	On the way back from visits	8
11	Other	6

Subjects reporting to be in prison for the first time were significantly more likely to report to have been bullied than other prisoners ($X^2 = 18.11$; p<.0001). 35.4 per cent of first time prisoners reported to have been bullied as compared to 14.2 per cent of other prisoners. This feature was consistent between the two prisons. In Prison A, 30.4 per cent reported to have been bullied as compared to 12.7 per cent of those who had been to prison previously. In Prison B, 43.2 per cent of first timers reported to have been bullied as compared to 17 per cent of other prisoners.

The small proportion of non-white prisoners in these surveys made assessment of racial bullying difficult, but 5 out of 9 Asian prisoners (55.6 per cent) and 4 out of 15 black prisoners (26.7 per cent) reported to have been bullied as compared to 20.3 per cent of white prisoners. The evidence that racial bullying is taking place is supported by the finding that "being called names about my colour" was selected by 7 prisoners in the survey and yet only 29 prisoners (9.3 per cent) identified themselves as being from black, asian or "other" ethnic origins.

Of 62 prisoners who reported to have been bullied, 36 (58.1 per cent) reported to feel safe at their current prison as compared to 89.5 per cent of those who had reported not to have been bullied. The association between feeling safe and not being bullied was highly significant ($X^2 = 33.39$; p<.00001).

The age of subjects and their home area did not appear to be related to bullying either as bullies or victims. Subjects from an urban region reported to have bullied and been bullied less than other groups but neither association was strong.

A correlation was found between length of time in prison and reporting to bully (r = .34; p<.001). Of 25 subjects who reported to have bullied, 21 (84 per cent) had been in prison over 6 weeks ($X^2 = 8.04$; p<.005). No such relationship was found for those reporting to be bullied (r = -.002; p>.9). Of 65 reporting to be victims of bullying 31 (47.7 per cent) had been in prison for less than 6 weeks.

No difference was found between the two prisons. At Prison A, prisoners who reported to have attended the induction course were less likely to report to have been bullied (16.4 per cent as compared to 28.1 per cent). At Prison B this effect was not found, but the number of prisoners reporting to have not attended was higher than expected. Only 27.6 per cent said they had attended.

Discussion

One in five prisoners reported to have been bullied in these two prisons. Of the two, more Prison B subjects reported to have been bullied than at Prison A, but the difference was not large (25.2 per cent as compared to 19.6 per cent). Similarly Prison B subjects were more likely to report to have bullied others than Prison A subjects (10.5 per cent as compared to 7.1 per cent).

The high proportion of those who report to have bullied and been bullied (40 per cent of bullies) warrants further exploration. Figures relating to length of stay (see below) and this finding may suggest that the relationship between bullying and being bullied is complex, but may be a process of adaptation into the prison culture. That is, new prisoners may be vulnerable to being "tested" on arrival, and a proportion of them may go on to bully others in their turn.

The survey did allow some assessment of who was likely to be bullied. From these results it appears that those people who report to be in prison for the first time are far more likely to report to having been bullied. This effect was particularly marked at Prison B where 43.2 per cent of those reporting to be in prison for the first time also reported to be bullied.

This finding can be explained in terms of returning prisoners having had opportunity to learn how to behave assertively in prison and not present themselves as vulnerable. First time prisoners are likely to appear unsure and anxious and may draw attention to themselves early in their prison stay. Additionally, prison officers report that bullying is regularly observed to begin with subtle actions, such as asking for a cigarette or teasing another prisoner and later escalating to more aggressive behaviours. This suggests that the initial actions of the "victim" may mediate the further actions of the "bully". This aspect may provide a basis for future research.

Another finding in this survey was that relating to length of time in prison and bullying. Subjects who had been in prison for longer were more likely to report to have bullied others, whereas no such relationship was found for reporting to have been bullied. Again this may relate to the point above, whereby new prisoners are more likely to be "tested out" on arrival, or during the early part of their stay, and it is likely to be an established prisoner who will confront them. Prisons may be regarded as unusual institutions in respect of the fact that prisoners are constantly arriving and departing and so establishing peer groups is more difficult than in schools or other institutions where the general pattern of arrival and departure is annual. Each new group of arrivals is small and likely to be vulnerable to the few established prisoners they are exposed to. It may also be possible that the longer stay prisoners in each prison are those more likely to have committed more serious crimes (e.g., those serving long sentences or those remanded in custody prior to longer Crown Court cases). The relationship between bullying and other delinquent behaviour is in need of further investigation.

The types of bullying reported in this survey demonstrate that a variety of behaviours are involved and there is evidence for suggesting that physical, verbal and psychological bullying all occur within the prison environment. The manipulative nature of prison bullying is demonstrated by the finding that "threatened" is the most commonly reported bullying both by bullies and victims. This suggests that much bullying in prison surrounds issuing threats in order to get someone to behave in a particular way. The fact that "having belongings taken" is also commonly reported indicates that much aggressive behaviour in prison is focused on the acquisition of goods. Other research in prisons has highlighted this aspect of prison bullying (e.g., Shine and Wilson, 1988) and the limited resources available to prisoners are likely to remain a source of competition.

The large proportion of prisoners reporting "racial name calling" as a form of bullying is a disturbing finding considering the small proportion of ethnic minority prisoners. The treatment of ethnic minority prisoners should be investigated further using methods which will allow us to compensate for small sample sizes.

The places where bullying is reported to happen are often highly supervised areas. Association is always organized with officers in attendance and reception is a unit where staff control the movement of prisoners in and out of the prison. This latter area is clearly important as a location, as bullying here is likely to set the expectations of the prisoner for the rest of his stay. The large number of reports of bullying occurring after lock-up time at night indicates that physically segregating prisoners in cells does not prevent them bullying each other verbally through their windows. Staff report that a common form of bullying at Prison B involves a prisoner being threatened with violence unless he sings a song out of his window. This form of public humilation does not require the bully and victim to be in physical contact but may clearly cause distress to the "victim".

The only effect that was found in only one of the prisons was that of the impact of an induction course. Both prisons keep newly arrived prisoners together for their first 24 hours, and both offer some sessions intended to ameliorate their transition into the prison system. Prison A's course includes a one hour session focused on bullying.

At Prison A, prisoners who reported to have attended the course were less likely to report to have been bullied. The course contains a session led by prison officers which discusses the effects of bullying on the individual and the institution, and attempts to discourage bullying.

At Prison B this effect was not found, but the number of prisoners reporting to have not attended was higher than expected.

This survey illustrates that there are groups of prisoners who are more likely to report to be bullied than others. Future strategies need to focus on aspects of vulnerability as well as monitoring changes in the situation, and other measures should be included to assess the reliability and validity of self-reports. It seems likely that the self-reporting of bullying of others is likely to be less reliable than the reporting of being bullied. This needs to be assessed in reference to staff reports and other data to provide a focus for strategy in reference to those bullying as well as those proving to be vulnerable.

Anti-bullying policy in prisons

Investigation of the behaviours reported by prison staff and prisoners to be involved in bullying led to the development of illustrative models to aid the understanding of bullying. It has become apparent that bullying comprises a range of varied behaviours and the following model was devised to illustrate this range.

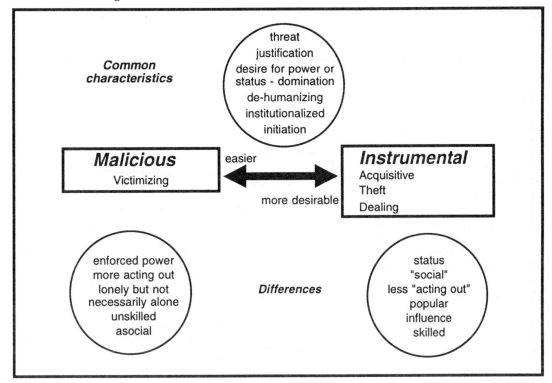

The "common characteristics" outlined in the above model are designed to illustrate some of the features which may be common to all episodes of bullying. Clearly, bullying involves an imbalance of power and threat is a key feature of maintenance in that imbalance. Such threats may include those which reduce the risks of detection such as threat of reprisal in the form of physical assault should staff be informed.

"Justification" and "dehumanizing" have been included to note the attempts made by those who bully to excuse their behaviour when challenged. These can be illustrated by comments made by prisoners such as "I wasn"t bullying him, I was only threatening him" (Tanner and Beck, Prison Service Psychology Conference Paper, 1993). Prisoners are also commonly reported to "target" vulnerable prisoners, many of whom will be given derogatory names such as "nonce" or "grass" in order to reduce their worth and status (Brookes, 1993). Such actions may help reduce any feelings of guilt that are felt by the attacker.

Other justifications include the minimizing of the impact of bullying behaviour. This may be reflected in the use of euphemistic descriptions of actions. Bunton describes a "game" called "Mallett"s Mallet" which is named after a children's TV programme. In the TV programme a contestant is hit with a soft rubber mallet when answering quiz questions wrongly. In the YOI version a new prisoner was followed into the shower where he was confronted with a "coded" question. If he answers wrongly (which he inevitably does) he is struck with a weapon such as a pool ball or PP9 battery in a sock. A further example was the reporting of an activity at a YOI called "helping with the shopping". This involves threatening a new prisoner on his visit to the canteen (prison shop) with reprisals unless he hands over his goods. McGurk and McDougall also describe an activity known as "the buzz" in which prisoners may be strangled until passing out. They point out that such activities could easily result in death.

The term "institutionalization" is included to highlight the appearance of bullying in a variety of social settings, such as the school or workplace. Bullying is not solely a problem among delinquent youths held in a penal institution. "Initiation" has been included to illustrate the finding that bullying is likely to occur close to arrival in a new setting. This may take the form of "testing out" the new person prior to further actions such as extortion and theft.

Among the differences are the levels of skill incorporated into the extreme forms of these behaviours. At one end, malicious acts of violence may take little planning, involve little effort to avoid detection and may reduce popularity among peers. At the opposite end of this spectrum is the sophisticated and "social" behaviour of group extortion, denial, avoidance of punishment and maintenance of control.

This model was then extended to incorporate the behaviours of those who are bullied and those who are not involved.

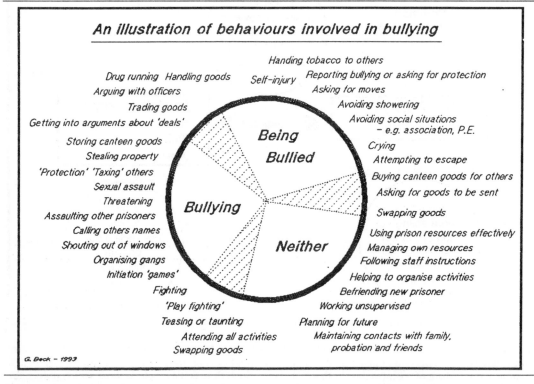

An illustration of behaviours involved in bullying

Handing tobacco to others
Drug running Handling goods   Self-injury   Reporting bullying or asking for protection
Arguing with officers   Asking for moves
Trading goods   Avoiding showering
Getting into arguments about 'deals'   Avoiding social situations
Storing canteen goods   – e.g. association, P.E.
                                               Crying
Stealing property   Attempting to escape
'Protection' 'Taxing' others   Buying canteen goods for others
Sexual assault   Asking for goods to be sent
Threatening
Assaulting other prisoners   Swapping goods
Calling others names
Shouting out of windows   Using prison resources effectively
Organising gangs   Managing own resources
Initiation 'games'   Following staff instructions
                                               Helping to organise activities
Fighting   Befriending new prisoner
'Play fighting'   Working unsupervised
Teasing or taunting   Planning for future
Attending all activities   Maintaining contacts with family,
Swapping goods   probation and friends

Being Bullied

Bullying

Neither

G. Beck – 1993

This is intended to demonstrate that, although bullying may be widely thought to involve some behaviours, others may be more ambiguous. It is also possible to engage in the bullying of others whilst being victimized, as seen in the results of the self reports described above. This model does not explain how behaviour varies, or indeed how it may be stable across situations as reported by Olweus (1978) and others in the research conducted in schools. More thorough research is needed to explain the persistence of bullying by some people, which may point to indicators concerning delinquency generally; and situational variation observed particularly in the prison setting. Such variability occurs in anecdotal reports from prison staff who may explain their observations by the existence and operation of a "natural hierarchy". An example of this is the removal of "vulnerable" prisoners who have been victimized to a "protected wing", where they are then accused of bullying others in that environment. The apparent "switch" from victim to bully (and perhaps back again shortly afterwards) merits investigation.

Other changes in behaviour that may provide a focus for further thought are the apparently pro-social behaviours that may precede acts of extortion. For example, Brookes (1993) notes that new prisoners often experience the kindness and generosity of established prisoners only to find that they are now heavily in debt and under threat to pay immediately. The "befriending" of prisoners is skilful and could be helpful to the running of the establishment ... but the exploitation of this skill is difficult to prevent.

The final model was developed to illustrate the variability of behaviours that may, or may not be, involved in bullying. In few cases will a person engage in solely bullying behaviour, but will be observed engaging in a variety of interactions. This illustrates the problem of categorizing people as "bully", "victim" or "neither", as a person may alter his or her behaviour to accommodate the demands of a particular social interaction. A simple example may include prisoners who are co-operative and polite with staff members but abusive and overbearing with their peers. Researchers have previously highlighted difficulties of categorization by adding categories of "provocative victim", "bully/victim" and "anxious bully" (Stephenson and Smith, 1989). Such categories do not allow explanation of the variability of behaviour between situations.

The "grey areas" were included to allow consideration of behaviours which may be ambiguous in terms of assigning to categories. Such ambiguity leads to problems when one considers that assertive, social leadership may involve behaviours that may also be labelled "bullying". Such recognition leads to the consideration of rewarding aspects of assertion and leadership (dominance) without wishing to extinguish the entire behavioural repertoire. This clearly has implications for the design of interventions or policies aiming to reduce the extent and severity of bullying.

Approaches to anti-bullying policy

For the sake of simplicity I will divide approaches into three categories. There will be other ways to divide any policies and interventions, and the three categories I have chosen will inevitably overlap, but my intention is to aid the development of policy which combats bullying using illustrative examples.

The three categories mentioned are:

1. Security and control;

2. Individual treatment and behaviour change;

3. Cultural and environmental change.

1. Security and control

This category comprises policies which aim to reduce the opportunity to bully. At its most extreme this would mean ensuring that prisoners did not ever meet in unsupervised situations for long enough to intimidate, threaten, or assault one another.

Practically, this approach has been widely used in prisons, from the fitting of light switches on the outside of dormitory walls to allow night staff to check on behaviour inside (McDougall and McGurk, 1986), to the fitting of CCTV in residential units and other areas suspected to be "high risk" locations (e.g., showers). Another application of this approach is in the development of a points system which allows staff to reduce or limit privileges when behavioural rules are broken.

This approach also advocates the removal of problematic prisoners, such as segregation for alleged bullying and removal to "vulnerable" or "protected" units for those who get bullied. One problematic feature of this approach, which is noted by staff, is that the role of the removed prisoner is swiftly filled by another in that location. This leads to the perpetuation of belief in a natural "pecking order" effect. This approach has a number of clear advantages and disadvantages compared to others.

Firstly, it enables the institution to adapt to new problems. Whenever a new bullying case comes to light, the circumstances can be assessed and new security measures put in place to prevent the re-occurrence of the problem.

Second, the staff of the institution can feel that their role is crucial in the prevention of bullying and so maintain a feeling of control and worthiness of their work. If staff are in the position of responsibility for ensuring that bullying does not occur, and are accountable as such, they are likely to ensure that bullying does not occur.

Third, is the simplicity of translating policy into practice. The policy says "reduce opportunities" and the practice involves the observation of behaviour and the intervention of staff whenever bullying is suspected. Disadvantages are also apparent however.

First, is the problem that prisoners adapt to the preventative measures placed before them. People engage in bullying because it is rewarding. How this is so may not always be obvious to those of us who work in institutions but the resilience of bullying behaviours and the reports of people who do bully indicate that there are gains to be made.

No matter what preventative measures are taken there will be opportunities to adapt. This might mean that overt acts of aggression are reduced, while the amount and severity of threats are increased. From this and previous research (Beck, unpublished), it is apparent that most bullying incidents are reported to involve threats rather than acts of physical violence. These threats can be issued through cell windows, over the servery, in a heavily supervised association period, in corridors etc. Threats can also allude to future violence which may not even be within the restrictions of the prison environment. An example is the issuing of threats to a member of the victim's family.

On a simpler level, if prisoners learn that a camera is set up to observe their behaviour in the canteen they will not offend there, but will find an opportunity to do so elsewhere. Unlike the situation in shops where the site of theft is fixed (i.e., at the place where the goods are on display), in bullying the "target" moves around as much as the thief.

A second disadvantage lies with the source of the responsibility for bullying. If we maintain a security based approach the responsibility belongs to prison staff. If a person is caught bullying he may well respond "well, you should stop me doing it", or a victim "why did you let him do that?". When we operate these measures those responses are legitimate.

Additionally, the institution may be taking on a bullying role. As the institution is more powerful than the prisoners held within it, it may be perpetuating the idea that power has to be enforced in order to maintain control. This may become the rationalization for future bullying: "I was only doing what the prison did to me".

2. Individual treatment and behaviour change

This type of policy is driven by the notion that bullying is executed by a deviant few on an unfortunate or "inadequate" few. Both groups can therefore benefit from behaviour modification.

Typical interventions might include elements of the following:

* Assertiveness training - teaching the principle of behaving in ways which respect the rights of others as well as those of yourself. This is in comparison with aggressiveness, respecting own rights and ignoring those of others; and passive behaviour which is the reverse.

* Social skills training - teaching ways of behaving in the company of others that improves communication ability and respect. Often this model begins with the identification of deficits which need improvement.

* Self-esteem enhancement - this might include a counselling approach, such as reinforcing positive statements about one's self, or more "behavioural" treatments such as taking part in activities which are novel and challenging and achievable.

* Anger management training - also a skills based approach; teaching about how anger operates and some methods for recognizing the build up of anger and preventing escalation.

* Empathy training - "talk therapy" intended to enhance the individual's understanding of the perspectives and feelings of others.

Clearly this approach is dependent on the correct identification of those engaging in bullying and those being bullied, and careful assessment of needs having been identified. The effectiveness of treatment will also be determined by the motivation of the "client" to take part.

On the first of these points, previous research (Beck, 1993) indicated that the association between reporting to be a bully and being identified as such by prison staff was poor. Although this is not conclusive evidence, it does indicate that identification of who is bullying is not simple, or likely to be effective. Part of the disparity in that research was suspected to be due to the differences in definitions of bullying used by staff and prisoners and staff. It may also be that skilful bullying involves avoiding detection.

Bullied others

Prisoners' reports

		No	Yes	
Staff reports	No	101	24	125 (88.7%)
	Yes	10	6	16 (11.3%)
		111 (78.7%)	30 (21.3%)	

$X^2 = 1.85$, p<.17

Having been bullied

Prisoners' reports

		No	Yes	
Staff reports	No	97	31	128 (90.8%)
	Yes	3	10	13 (9.2%)
		100 (70.9%)	41 (29.1%)	

$X^2 = 13.44$, p<.0005

The second point above is concerned with the evaluation of treatment. Although the "rewards" of bullying may not always be obvious, they exist, and treatment does not necessarily provide new ways of satisfying those needs. Detection of bullying is difficult, (see above), and evaluation of treatment is dependent on detection.

The individual "tailoring" of treatment according to needs also indicates that bullying is not a singular behavioural response. Some bullies may require anger management training, but it may be that bullies are rarely angry ... if bullying involves getting what you want when you want it, why should you be angry about anything?

Similarly, enhancing self-esteem may seem an appropriate treatment when we believe that part of the decision to bully others involves feeling bad about oneself. However, the obvious result may be to leave the bullying behaviour unchanged and make the person feel better about himself.

The third point is concerned with motivation and consent. People who victimize others do so for a variety of positive rewards (discussed at length elsewhere). It seems unlikely that someone who is good at bullying should want to stop doing so, especially if the message from other prisoners and the institution is that you either bully or get bullied. This may be additionally reinforced by the institutional rules and routines. For example, low rates of pay amplify the importance of currency. The allocation of individuals according to the institution's needs creates a sense of "sink or swim", providing contingencies for the "sinker" does not remove the original message.

In terms of responsibility, this approach is superior to the security approach, at least in terms of being placed with (problematic) prisoners. Unfortunately, it only goes so far as to place it with those prisoners who are identified as being involved. When asked to identify those involved in bullying, staff at Feltham indicated that 12 per cent were involved as "bullies" and about the same proportion as victims. These were underestimates, and in most cases were the wrong people according to self reports by prisoners (Beck, 1993).

3. Cultural and environmental change

The basis for this type of policy is the notion that the environment of a prison could be designed in such a way that individuals do not wish to engage in bullying and are rewarded by engaging in co-operative ventures. This needs to involve the development of community involvement, the reward of social action and the development of responsibility. This approach is related to the "whole school approach" as advocated by a number of researchers working within the schools' environment (e.g., Olweus).

A basis for this approach is the notion that *everyone* in the institution is involved with bullying as with all institutional delinquency. From this research, around 30 per cent of prisoners reported that they had either bullied, been bullied (or both). This is likely to be an underestimate of the true figure, and we must consider the role of the rest. They are involved as either witnesses, bystanders, provocateurs or informers. The "whole prison" policy may include aspects of security and treatment approaches but will be more concerned with reducing competition between prisoners and rewarding co-operation and respect for others.

The disadvantage of this category of approach is that it demands more of the staff and management of institutions as they have to be highly imaginative to translate the policy into action, and to increase the accountability of prisoners by reducing the power of staff. It also demands constant attention to prevent "accidental" rewarding of delinquency.

Conclusions

I began this paper by suggesting that we should not be surprised that bullying occurs in young offender institutions. The people who are sent there by the courts have mostly been apprehended for offences of theft, robbery and violence, all of which may be associated with other forms of bullying.

Imprisonment is also an unusual and emotive experience, particularly for the first time, and the conditions of the system may accentuate strengths and weaknesses among the population. Resources are limited, competition strong and inevitably the mechanisms in place within prisons cannot cater for all eventualities. Constraints are tempered by the efforts of management and staff to continually improve our methods of combatting bullying. National initiatives include the recent release of a booklet giving advice on bullying strategies for governors, and many prisons have set up working groups to monitor the behaviour of the prisoners in their establishment. Such groups frequently request information from the research bases within the system.

Research in prisons has highlighted similarities and differences with the situation in schools and the workplace. It seems likely that bullying is an insidious and almost inevitable component of prison life and sometimes reduces prison staff to the time worn expression "it will never be stopped completely". Such comments arise from the frustration of working within a system that has competing functions and concerns. A clear conflict occurs when those working within the prison system confuse the punishment of the courts (imprisonment) with the punishment of the prisons. When this occurs, the statement of purpose we all strive to remember is jeopardized. I have not discussed bullying which may occur between prison staff members, or between prisoners and staff (in either direction). This is because there is no research to my knowledge which systematically explores this sensitive area.

What does seem clear is that bullying can vary from malicious acts of violence or threat "for the sheer pleasure of the act" to organized extortion by gangs. Violence may be disguised in the language of games or euphemisms and be an apparently embedded feature of the prison culture, for example, in initiation "ceremonies" described in the literature (McGurk and McDougall, 1986, 1991, 1993).

Despite the fact that our knowledge about bullying is expanding rapidly, our strategies for combatting it are varied and sometimes conflicting. This is a reflection of the recent increase in concern and motivation to improve the conditions and the influences of prison. The attribution of suicides and other self-harm to bullying has highlighted the seriousness of the effects of bullying and focused the attention of management on dealing with the problem.

It seems unlikely that interventions that have been in place for short periods of time will be able to alter the culture of a prison, but the efforts of the service to do so should be respected. Careful evaluation and monitoring is needed to assess the impact of efforts over the coming years.

Recommendations for future research

1. The finding that longer term prisoners are more likely to report to bullying others necessitates longitudinal research within the prison setting. It may be hypothesized that many of those who are bullied early in their prison stay go on to bully others later in their stay. Such a finding would suggest that prisoners could be encouraged to co-operate with new prisoners throughout their stay (for example, by providing opportunities for established prisoners to introduce newcomers to the prison within the structure of an induction course, under the supervision of staff), or alternatively to ensure that new prisoners are kept away from established prisoners during the early part of their stay.

2. Information regarding prisoners' offending behaviour should be maintained with a record of involvement in bullying. Should a relationship be found then prisoners may be allocated to activities according to offence characteristics, limiting the opportunity for people who are more likely to bully from having access to more vulnerable prisoners.

3. The experience of ethnic minority prisoners warrants further investigation. In particular, the reaction of staff members when racial bullying is witnessed should be assessed. It may be hypothesized that staff do not define bullying consistently and so may respond with appropriate interventions in some cases but not others.

4. Self-reports about bullying need to be corroborated with information from other sources. In previous research, prisoners identified as bullying by staff did not correspond with self-reported bullying (Beck, 1992). Interventions and strategies that depend upon identification of bullies should be given the best opportunities to identify them.

5. Interventions based on self-report surveys need to be evaluated in terms of their impact. At prison A in the current study, first time prisoners are now identified in the reception procedure and this is recorded in the local information system. Such prisoners are to be given extra training in their induction period which is intended to reduce the risk of being bullied. If this training aids their ability to cope this may be extended to other establishments. The effect on their involvement in bullying also needs to be assessed.

The attendance on the induction course may be recorded in a register to ensure that the self-reported attendance is correct.

References

BECK, G. (1992, unpublished) Bullying among incarcerated young offenders. MSc Research Paper submitted to Birkbeck College, University of London, MSc Applied Criminological Psychology

BESAG, V. (1989) **Bullies and Victims in Schools**. Milton Keynes, Open University Press

BROOKES, M. (1993, unpublished) Reducing Bullying at HMP Ranby. Report for Management

BUNTON, J. B. (1992) Bullying in prisons: a preliminary investigation into the possible role of personality characteristics in bullying behaviour among juvenile prisoners in a young offender population. Unpublished BSc thesis. Brunel University, Human Sciences Department

FARRINGTON, D. P. (1993) Understanding and preventing bullying. In Tonry and Morris (Eds) **Crime and Justice: An Annual Review of Research, Vol 17.** Chicago: University of Chicago Press

LANE, D. A. (1989) Bullying in school: the need for an integrated approach. **School Psychology International, 10,** 3, 211-215

LOWENSTEIN, L. F. (1978) Who is the bully? **Bulletin of the British Psychological Society, 31,** 147-149

HOME OFFICE (1992, unpublished) Prison Department, Directorate of Inmate Programmes. Summary of Research Findings, YOI research

MARSHALL, R. E. (1993) The application of psychological principles to the problem of bullying amongst young offenders: a multi-disciplinary approach. **Inside Psychology, The Journal of Prison Service Psychology,** 1, 2

McGURK, B. J., and McDOUGALL, C. (1986) The prevention of bullying among incarcerated delinquents. **DPS Report: Series 11,** No. 144. Also published in Thompson and Smith (1991), (Eds) **Practical Approaches to Bullying.** London. David Fulton and (1992) **Inside Psychology, 1,** 1

OLWEUS, D. (1984) Aggressors and their victims: bullying at school. In N. Frude and A. Gault (Eds) **Disruptive Behaviour in Schools.** New York: Wiley

OLWEUS, D. (1984) Stability in aggressive and withdrawn, inhibited behaviour patterns. In Kaplan, Konecni and Novaco (Eds) **Aggression in Children and Youth.** NATO/ASI Series. Martins Nijhoff Publishers

OLWEUS, D. (1978) **Aggression in the Schools: Bullies and Whipping Boys.** Washington DC: Hemisphere

OLWEUS, D. (1989) Bully/victim problems among school children: basic facts and effects of a school based intervention program. In Rubin and Peplar (Eds) (1991) **The Development and Treatment of Childhood Aggression.** Hillsdale, NJ: Erlbaum

PERRY, D. G., KUSEL, S. J., and PERRY, C. L. (1988) Victims of peer aggression. **Developmental Psychology, 24,** 807-814

ROLAND, E. (1989) Bullying: the Scandanavian research tradition. In D. P. Tattum and D. A. Lane (1989) **Bullying in Schools.** Stoke on Trent: Trentham Books

SHINE, J., and WILSON, P. (1988) Bullying and baroning activities. Unpublished report for management at a YOI in England, 3 October 1988

SMITH, P. K. (1991) The silent nightmare: bullying and victimization in school peer groups. **The Psychologist, 12,** 4, 243-248

TATTUM, D. P., and LANE, D. A. (1989) **Bullying in Schools.** Stoke on Trent: Trentham Books

TATTUM, D. P., and HERBERT, G. (1990) **Bullying - A Positive Response.** South Glamorgan Institute of Higher Education

Consent, coercion and culpability

Sarah Skett*

This paper examines two issues, namely, consent to treatment when placed within a criminal justice setting, and that of innocence and degree of culpability of individuals sentenced to custodial terms. The problems presented by these two very real ethical dilemmas are brought into the open and discussed on a pragmatic level, with reference to clinical experience and relevant literature. It concludes that for both of these issues there needs to be an acknowledgement of a wide range of issues that are perhaps at present not tackled within existing codes of conduct, and not discussed openly and fully in a professional context. In addition, frameworks are suggested in order to address and discuss professional clinical practice, with a view to giving it more emphasis.

Consent

Consent to treatment is a fundamental part of The British Psychological Society's Code of Conduct. Within the criminal justice system this becomes a very difficult issue, with many writers agreeing with Metzner (1993) in insisting prison is inherently coercive.

Coercive regimes

The life sentence. The life sentence is split into two parts; the term to be served in order to effect retribution or punishment, and the period after this term has been completed, where the life sentence prisoner must prove they are no longer a threat to society. The threat or "risk" to the community is assessed initially after sentence with reference to factors related to the offence. This assessment is partly behavioural, and partly based on interview. All lifers have regular reviews or F75 reports with a major review occurring just before the period of punishment is completed. If the Home Office is not then satisfied that the risk posed by releasing the individual is acceptable, they will not allow release to take place, and will set another review date. In addition, there are discretionary and mandatory life sentences. The latter is the only sentence available to the courts for murder. The former is imposed on those individuals convicted of other crimes of sufficient seriousness to warrant a life sentence (for example, arson, sex offences, or manslaughter). The two sentences are handled differently, especially with regard to the mechanism whereby individuals can be released. For mandatory life sentence prisoners, their case is reviewed by the Local Review Committee and ultimately the Home Secretary. The discretionary life sentence prisoner is more fortunate in that their potential release is reviewed by a tribunal which has legal standing, and which hears evidence for and against release.

What do lifers have to do to prove they are no longer a threat to society? During the initial few years of sentence, their behaviour is assessed to give a series of risk factors present at the time of the offence. These can range from situational (for example criminal lifestyle), to individual (for example, temper or alcohol problems). Over the next few years lifers are then expected to prove they have addressed these risk factors. It is on this that the final release agreement rests; i.e. that the risk factors present at the time of the offence have been significantly reduced or removed. Inevitably this involves some form of psychological intervention and treatment. If individuals do not take part in the system, decline to co-operate, do not agree with official assessments of their offence, refuse to address risk

---

* The views expressed in this paper are those of the author, and not the Home Office, Prison Service, or institution.

factors, or refuse to accept the validity of treatments offerred, they will not progress smoothly towards release.

This does not provide an environment within which the individual can freely choose whether to consent to treatment or not. Therefore, as psychologists working within the prison system we are often unable to assess whether or not we are adhering to the Code of Conduct, as it is presently written within The British Psychological Society's document (1985).

Sentence planning. Recent guidelines issued regarding the development of sentence planning for determinate sentence prisoners (a process whereby inmates risk factors for offending provide the basis for the activities encouraged throughout their sentence), make explicit the fact that if targets are not reached, or if an inmate does not co-operate with the system, then parole may be refused. The first refusals of parole to occur because of an inmate failing to co-operate were issued in 1993. Inmates are also being refused home leave because they have not attended the relevant (and in some cases irrelevant) offending behaviour groups. This is explicit coercion.

Is coercion good or bad?

The reasoning behind such coercion is perceived to be for the moral good; the protection of society by insisting prisoners address their risk of re-offending before being allowed back into the community. However, in order to have predictive validity for lower risk once released, whether on termination of sentence or on licence, courses must be evaluated and proven to be worthwhile; not only effective as an intervention but also acceptable to the inmate. This is not the case in most institutions. Further, if inmates perceive certain hoops through which they must jump to gain privileges, home leaves, parole and so on, many issues follow from this:

* How do we distinguish genuine motivation to change? This becomes important because degree of motivation affects treatment outcomes. Prochaska and DiClemente (1986) have shown there are different stages of change, ranging from believing there is no problem, thinking there is a problem but not willing or able to tackle it, to actively seeking alternatives. They suggest that any intervention package should tackle this as a fundamental issue in its design. Intuitively, it makes sense to tailor a package to the stage of change the client has reached.

* What effect do those who are present in the group for alternative motives have on its dynamics, as these depend on a healthy bonding and challenging of cognitive distortions? Group influence can swing both ways. On the one hand there is the possibility that those individuals who genuinely want to learn and change their behaviour may influence those who do not, or at least provide a challenging situation to those who are denying responsibility for their crimes and behaviour. The National Sex Offender Treatment Groups are based around this idea of inmates who are further towards taking full responsibility for their actions challenging those who have not. On the other hand, those inmates of dubious motivation may sabotage the group and influence or intimidate the better motivated inmates.

* There is little point in insisting someone attends a group when this will, in reality, do nothing to affect risk. Alternatively, it is possible to assess risk by the effect of of his or her behaviour on the group; therefore the attendance does serve a purpose, albeit not the one originally intended.

* What effect will the presence of unmotivated people have on evaluations and investigations as to effectiveness of interventions? Hollin (1993), in summarizing recent meta-analytic reviews of evaluative studies, points out that indiscriminant targeting of treatment programmes is counterproductive in reducing recidivism. However, anecdotal evidence from the Sex Offender Treatment Programme, seems to suggest that even those who are openly attending against their will, (i.e. denying guilt) do benefit in terms of taking responsibility for their actions.

In addition to these arguments, there is also the fact that, as therapists and professionals engaged in rehabilitative exercises, we often have to confront offenders with what they have done in order to achieve clinical progress. This is particularly the case for offenders who appear to actively suppress feelings of guilt and responsibility in order to continue offending. Many offenders do not actively agree to therapy because they do not consider there is anything wrong with them or their behaviour. We could therefore invoke the same arguments that are used to justify the Sectioning, under the Mental Health Act, of those deemed so mentally ill that they are a danger either to themselves or others.

Many drug rehabilitation programmes in the US are compulsory; often an individual is committed to the programme instead of receiving a custodial sentence. The argument here is the same as above in that many drug users do not consider they have a problem and therefore do not seek treatment. Programmes were made compulsory because it was perceived that the ethical questions involved were less important than the social and individual costs of drug use. It was emphasized that many crimes committed are related to drug use in some way, for example, those committed under their influence or in order to acquire the means to buy them.

However, several writers have pointed out that these practices were thinly veiled attempts at social control rather than social improvement (Rosenthal, 1988), highlighted by the fact that assessments of dangerousness or criminality were very rarely included (Sowers and Daley, 1993), and that individuals could be detained if they were deemed in danger of becoming dependent on drug use without any corresponding criminal or dangerous behaviour being evident (Tancredi, 1987).

What is the justifiable amount of coercion or challenging in getting someone to admit responsibility for their actions and recognize the consequences for their victims, and then to get them to accept they need help? Even this statement is overtly oppressive in that it imposes a moral framework on the behaviour of others. It presupposes that certain behaviours are "bad" and should be eradicated. One could argue that this is obviously the case with regard to serious actions such as violence against the person, but what of other areas that are rather less distinct? One example might be the medicalization of homosexuality, where only a few decades ago gay men were deemed sick and in need of treatment. How far do we go in our forcible and coercive behaviour? How do we know when to draw the line between acceptable and not acceptable? What degree of coercion and confrontation is acceptable, given that some is inevitable within the criminal justice system?

The imbalance of power

It is possible that coercion is present within the criminal justice system because of the inherent imbalance of power; inmates are perceived, and perceive themselves, to have little or no power over their fate whilst in prison. The authorities are perceived to have all the power with which to make decisions and therefore force people to behave in various ways. In general, the more co-operative an inmate, the better he or she will fare within the system. In a sense this is a microcosm of society at large, where the same holds true. Conformity, to a large extent, is desired; rebellion, revolution and non-conformity are not, except under exceptional circumstances.

Gale (1994), goes further in echoing these sentiments by suggesting inherent within psychology is the tendency to support the status quo, by convincing and coercing - "helping" - individuals to accept established society and its rules and regulations. A good example would be the recent establishment response to the travelling population, where a group of individuals have rejected the society on offer and attempted to create their own way of life. This has led to confrontation with the general public and the authorities.

Definition of consent

We should also consider our definition of consent. Within the medical establishment this definition has changed dramatically over the last forty years (*New Scientist*, 1994). Initially it represented simply agreeing with your doctor as to the best course of treatment. Later it evolved into presenting information to enable a choice to be made by the patients themselves. Currently it seems to be changing again so that individuals are required to demonstrate that they understand the issues involved before making a decision.

When applied to a psychological intervention within a penal establishment, I feel we are still operating under the initial medical definition of the client simply agreeing with the professional because "they know best". To engender greater choice we should be explaining the possible side-effects of therapy, what it would mean to undergo it, how the person can expect to feel half-way through, and what implications it has for the future. As we all know, these facts will not necessarily be positive. Some people tend to feel worse in the middle of a set of therapy sessions than they do before and after; teaching someone to become assertive may have wide ranging implications for existing relationships with family and friends; and convincing someone never to take drugs again may lead to them feeling alienated and lonely because they reject, or are rejected by, their drug taking peer group. In order to allow people to make choices for themselves it is only fair to give them the information they need.

Conclusion

It is hoped that by bringing these issues out into the open we can consider their implications and their possible resolutions in our everyday work. We must provide a service to society that is based on sound ethical principles, one that we can justify and defend. As psychologists within the penal system, our role is to provide a professional ethical overview to a situation which could quite easily swing too far towards the oppressive and coercive. We have to be careful that we do not generate the view that because offenders have broken the law they are then not entitled to the same treatment rights as any other clients. This is in no way to negate or minimize their offences or the devastating affect criminal behaviour can have on its victims. For the greater good it is better to keep offenders in jail until they are safe to release than to offer them their rights to consent to treatment without penalizing the decision to refuse. From a utilitarian point of view the wellbeing of the many always outweighs the wellbeing of the individual. Common sense decrees that we do not release violent offenders unless they have been rehabilitated.

Consent to treatment has to be balanced by the need to protect the public from violence and to encourage offenders to address their behaviour. Getting this balance right is an enormous task, and one which is perhaps ignored as being either too difficult or not in fact a real issue in many establishments.

As professionals we ought to challenge unethical behaviour when we see it and develop alternative strategies based on agreed professional standards and the context of working within the criminal justice system. Where, then, is the dividing line between acceptable and unacceptable behaviour for professionals and institutions? I believe we all need to engage in dialogue and debate in order to determine, if not an answer to this question, a set of operational guidelines that are pragmatic and useful in every day practice.

Culpability

Prisons treat everyone committed to them by the courts precisely because they have been committed by the courts. This presupposes that the courts are infallible. As we have seen recently, this is far from the case. Public faith has been rocked by the series of highly publicized miscarriages of justice. Names such as the Birmingham Six, the Guildford Four, and the Cardiff Three have challenged the traditional view that the British Judicial System is sound. Many people serving long sentences have to wait an inordinate amount of time for their appeals to be heard, assuming they will actually proceed to a formal hearing and not falter at the first hurdle of review. Even when a person is granted leave to appeal, in order to assess guilt or the degree of culpability of the individual, there is no guarantee justice will prevail.

The possibility of innocence

It is possible, therefore, that psychologists within the prison system will sooner or later encounter individuals who are innocent of the crimes of which they were convicted. Assuming that this is the case, what are the implications? Once an individual has been committed by the courts to a term of imprisonment, there is little support for them in claiming their innocence, even taking into account the appeals procedure. As stated above, the prison authorities are forced to treat the individual as guilty; they are given no other choice. In addition, there are many biases from which none of us is immune. For example:

* the tendency to make fundamental attribution errors, where one overestimates the degree to which the person is responsible for certain occurrences, and underestimates the effect of situational factors;

* the tendency to believe there is no smoke without fire, i.e. to justify a person's presence within the prison system by insisting that "there must be something in it";

* the tendency to place trust in the legal institutions of this country so that it becomes uncomfortable and unnerving to admit they might have got it wrong.

For a fuller discussion of these biases see Fitzmaurice and Pease (1986).

Imprisonment of innocent individuals must have a profound effect. One most obvious effect is that of the self-fulfilling prophecy; this can work two ways:

* when an institution such as the prison service is forced both by the establishment and by human bias to assume everyone is guilty, it will start to observe behaviour commensurate with the criminal it believes the individual to be;

* individuals may start to view life in a self-destructive way by behaving in the manner in which they believe the authorities expect of them. There have been many occasions in my own experience when interviewing prisoners, where I have heard them say "I'll give them something to put me in prison for".

The net result is to both produce and notice behaviour which would be expected of an individual who was guilty of the crime of which he or she was convicted. Risk assessment and identification of offending behaviour become difficult, as no information to work on is supplied or can be supplied by the individual, and, as stated above, there is the danger of a self-fulfilling prophecy, where risk factors are identified from the details of the offence supplied by the records and concomitant behaviour is sought. If you look long enough and hard enough you will find the behaviour required.

Innocence becomes a difficult problem for the psychologist to deal with. How do you know whether the person is merely denying the offence or really is innocent? Such a fundamental decision should not have to be made, nor are we qualified to make it, but in practice it is almost forced upon us. Further, having decided there is reasonable doubt as to the validity of the conviction, what can you do; what ought you to do? There is a fundamental ethical problem to be tackled here: one of justice. If as a psychologist you are convinced there is doubt over a conviction, justice insists that you try to do something to assist the individual and redress the balance. However, even this could be contrary to the client's best interests, as it increases the possibility of others concluding there is a degree of collusion by the professional, or manipulation on behalf of the inmate, therefore leading to him or her appearing as an even higher risk.

Employees of the prison service have no voice with which to raise concerns; we are actively encouraged not to get involved with individuals whose guilt is in doubt. The reasoning behind this is clear: as workers we are not qualified to make this decision as we are not judicially or legally trained, and therefore cannot adequately judge a person's actions. This is true, but it does not solve the problem raised when we are faced with the protestations of a prisoner that he or she is innocent.

Innocence or denial?

Denial of the offence can be viewed in two ways. As stated above, denial is often viewed as a significant risk factor: the offender is refusing to come to terms with the crime and admit responsibility. If this continues over an entire life sentence, the authorities will be much less likely to agree to release, as no risk factors will have been addressed. How do we assess the relative likelihood of the prisoner being innocent or simply in denial? Should we be making such a judgement at all? If we decide in favour of innocence, what next?

Degree of culpability

There is also degree of culpability to take into account. Innocence is not necessarily a dichotomous variable. For example, individuals can be found guilty of murder "by association" where they did not actually commit the final act of murder, but were significantly involved in the events leading up to it. How do we treat protestations of innocence in this case? It now becomes easier to assess behaviour, produce risk factors, and address them, even though the inmate insists he or she should not be serving a life sentence for murder, as there are sufficient circumstances to warrant concern. Further, a criminal or delinquent lifestyle may have been a factor in calling the individual to the attention of the police, even though he or she is innocent of the index offence.

Risk assessment can take on a much wider perspective not necessarily directly related to the crime. Inmates still have to take part in the life of the institution, thus providing information on which to base a decision of risk. For example, an inmate insisting his or her innocence may still be a violent, volatile individual, with many assaults on others within the institution, who might benefit from psychological intervention.

Conclusion

The Royal Commission on Criminal Justice (1991-3) recommended that an independent review body be instigated to provide support and advice to prisoners who believe their conviction is unfair. It would seem wholly sensible to extend access to this body to the workers within the criminal justice system, to give them support and advice in a very complex and difficult situation, and to allow them to articulate concerns they may have about an individual's conviction.

It is important to treat all inmates with the same degree of professionalism regardless of whether they insist they are innocent. As forensic psychologists we can support people psychologically whilst they contest their convictions, we can structure expectations and explain the system to enable people to make choices as to their course of action, and we can, in some instances, still carry out our function as risk assessors, depending on the circumstances of the offence.

However, we must keep in mind our ethical position, and take every opportunity to discuss and mediate solutions to potential problems. We must never push aside such questions and we must never become complacent as to our position within the criminal justice system.

References

NEW SCIENTIST (1994) In the name of consent (editorial). 19 February

FITZMAURICE and PEASE (1986) **The Psychology of Judicial Sentencing.** Manchester: Manchester University Press

GALE, A. (1994) Do we need to think a bit more about ethical issues? **DCLP Newsletter, 37**

HOLLINS, C. (1993) Advances in the treatment of delinquent behaviour. **Criminal Behaviour and Mental Health, 3,** 142-157

METZNER, J. L. (1993) Guidelines for psychiatric services in prison. **Criminal Behaviour and Mental Health, 3,** 252-267.

PROCHASKA, J. O., and DiCLEMENTE (1986) Toward a comprehensive model of change. In Miller and Heather (Eds) **Treating Addictive Behaviour: Processes of Change.** New York: Plenum

ROSENTHAL, M. P. (1988) The constitutionality of involuntary civil commitment of opiate addicts. **The Journal of Drug Issues, 18,** 641-661

ROYAL COMMISSION ON CRIMINAL JUSTICE (1991-3) (Led by Lord Runciman) **Report. Cm. 2263.** London: HMSO

SOWERS, W. E., and DALEY, D. C. (1993) Compulsory treatment of substance use disorders. **Criminal Behaviour and Mental Health, 3,** 403-415

TANCREDI, L. R. (1987) Commitment of non-criminal addicts: where does it stand? **Psychiatric Medicine, 3,** 253-266

Criminal prediction scores and survival analysis

John B. Copas

Prediction scores for parole have usually been for a fixed time horizon, for example, the parole score developed by the Home Office estimates the probability of a reconviction within two years. When a variable time horizon is needed such as envisaged in the new Criminal Justice Act, a predictor is required on a sliding scale to allow for the different periods of potential parole. The natural statistical setting for developing such a predictor is survival analysis. Survival analysis consists of estimating "survival curves", S(t) = Probability (no reconviction by time t). The survival curve for each individual is derived from an estimate of that individual's "hazard function" or instantaneous rate of offences or convictions. The paper describes this approach as applied to criminological data.

Introduction

There are several examples in the criminal justice system of the use of statistical prediction scales in providing guidance to decision makers. Perhaps the best known is the Reconviction Prediction Score which has been used by the Parole Board in England and Wales. This score, constructed from data from a large sample of subjects in the late 1960s, provides a percentage figure for the likelihood of a reconviction within two years of release from prison (Nuttall et al., 1977). Other examples of statistical scales are the Cambridgeshire Risk of Reconviction Scale (Merrington, 1990), a scale for probationers (Humphrey et al., 1991), and the Sentence Prediction Scale of Fitzmaurice (1991).

The use of such scales seems to be positively encouraged by the new Criminal Justice Act. The 1991 Act urges that decision making be more systematic and more accountable. Although other considerations are clearly involved, it is envisaged that "The decision whether to allow parole should be based first and foremost on considerations of risk of serious harm to the public" (1990 White Paper "Crime, Justice and Protecting the Public", p.33). Further, the evaluation of this risk needs to be made on a clearly defined set of available factors which are "indicative of the likelihood of reoffending". The logical limit of this quest for more systematic ways of evaluating risk is that the risk assessment should be expressed on a numerical scale, and that its value should be capable of being calculated from a well-defined set of risk indicators. In other words, a statistical predictor. This was indeed envisaged by the 1988 Carlisle Report, which stated that "the Parole Board should be under a duty to take into account statistical prediction techniques ... which will assist in its work".

It is precisely this systematic and arithmetical nature of statistical prediction scores which has led many decision-makers to express reservations about their use in practice. If statistical scores are to be accepted and used, it is worth exploring what lies behind such misgivings. There seem to be (at least) two main reasons, one obvious and the other more subtle.

Firstly, there can be a lack of clarity between the statements that the *assesment of risk* should be systematic, and that the *decison* should be systematic. Few would argue for the latter; bodies responsible for decision-making have generally rejected the idea of imposing rigid thresholds so that, for example, everyone whose score falls short of some particular figure should be automatically granted parole and everyone exceeding it should be refused. Thus the Carlisle Report, quoted above, went on to say: "By their nature statistical predictions can never be a substitute for the exercise of human judgement but they do provide value guidance on the question of risk".

Secondly, there is the question of the interpretation of a statistical predictor. One possibility, the "hard" interpretation, envisages a predictor as a behavioural model. For example, a prediction score of 30 per cent amounts to a model asserting that this particular individual will act as if he tosses a loaded coin, loaded to give a 30 per cent chance of heads and a 70 per cent chance of tails. He offends if and only if heads is obtained. The difficulty with such a model is that it can never be complete, and is always open to the criticism, "how can this predictor be reliable when it does not allow for ...". Even when a particular factor is taken into account, its role is usually tempered by hidden assumptions such as linearity in a chosen coding scheme, or additivity (no interaction) with other factors. The hard interpretation may be acceptable to statisticians who are used to thinking in terms of probability models, but it is not, it is argued, an appropriate vehicle for commending prediction scales to decision-makers.

An alternative view of prediction scores, the "soft" interpretation, is that they are nothing more or less than descriptions of what has been observed in the past. According to this interpretation, a prediction score is not a model for the behaviour of the particular individual, but amounts to a note of the offending experience of a set of individuals in the past who, on a clearly stated set of risk indicators, matches the subject in question. This idea is explored in more detail in the next section: briefly, a prediction score is a system of labelling risk groups, the labels being calibrated in some meaningful way, for example as the proportion of reconvictions in two years, or, in Section 3, as the survival curve expressing the pattern of offending over time. The soft interpretation is entirely consistent with the previously stated view that a prediction score is a way of expressing relevant information to decision-makers, rather than as a trigger for any particular decision outcome.

Risk groups and labels

A statistical predictor, by its very nature, combines together the values of a set of indicator factors into a single score. It thus defines a collection of "risk groups", each group consisting of those individuals who share a common value for the score. The predictor will have been fitted to a (hopefully large) set of individuals in the past, all of whom will have been followed up to monitor offences or convictions. The risk groups can be identified in such data, and their offending records determined. One risk group will have offended relatively frequently, another group may have a very low level of offending, with most groups somewhere in between. The score acts as a label for such risk groups, and as a link between an individual in question and a particular risk group which has been observed in the past. For example, returning to the score of 30 per cent, this score merely asserts that, on the basis of the set of indicators involved, the individual in question is a member of a risk group of whom 30 per cent have been observed to reoffend (in the sense envisaged by the score) in the past. In a particular case the score may be "wrong" in the sense that the decision-maker may know some other feature which makes reoffending for this individual virtually certain, or extremely unlikely, but it cannot be consistently "wrong" since the figure of 30 per cent has been observed for the risk group as a whole.

The success of a prediction score is seen in terms of how widely differentiated are the offending rates across the risk groups. The ideal score is one which defines only two risk groups: one in which offending always occurs, and the other in which it never occurs. Such a degree of polarization can never be obtained in practice; the most that can be hoped for is a reasonably wide spread of offence rates over the range 0 per cent to 100 per cent. A simple (and also simple-minded) way of assessing a prediction score is to imagine asserting that an individual will offend if his score exceeds 50 per cent and asserting that he will not offend if his score is less than 50 per cent. The "per cent correctly classified" is then the overall percentage of correct assertions. If the offending rates of the risk groups are exactly uniformly distributed over the range 0 per cent to 100 per cent, then the "percentage correctly classified" turns out to be 75 per cent. In most applications the distribution of offending rates over the risk groups is unimodal and so the "percentage correctly classified" is somewhat lower - for the Home Office's Reconviction Prediction Score (Nuttall et al., 1977), for example, it is about 69 per cent.

The object of a statistical prediction scale is to define an effective set of risk groups. Once these are set up, their labelling is essentially arbitrary. Manheim and Wilkins (1955, p.146) defined five risk groups for reoffending after borstal training, which they labelled A, B, X, C and D. Copas and Whitely (1976) had four risk groups for psychopaths entering a therapeutic community - which they labelled "poor", "below average", "above average" and "good". The convention has now arisen, however, that labels should be *calibrated* in terms of the percentage reoffending (or whatever follow-up criterion is envisaged).

In practice many prediction scales in criminology have used the point-scoring method of Burgess (1928). The method is particularly simple, and consists of adding a series of increments, each increment being the difference between the offending rate observed for that particular level of a factor

which pertains to the individual in question, and the overall offending rate. Two of the n̠
Home Office's Reconviction Prediction Score (Nuttall et al., 1977), for example, are shown in Ta̠

Adding over some dozen or so increments produces a total score. These values of the total score ar̠
then calibrated against the actual reoffending rates which have been observed in the past for risk
groups defined by those total scores. Figure 1 shows a typical calibration graph. The usual procedure
is to fit a straight line through the points on the calibration graph, which then defines a simple linear
conversion of the total score to a percentage rate of reoffending.

Although intuitively appealing and simple to calculate, the Burgess method, with the resulting linear
calibration, is not a statistically optimum procedure, and more recent methods using logistic
regression are often more powerful (Collet, 1991; Dobson, 1990). Another important statistical issue is
that of "shrinkage", the tendency for the reoffending rates of risk groups which may be observed in
the future to be differentiated somewhat less clearly than the reoffending rate calibrated against the
original data on which the score was constructed. Ideally the calibration of risk groups needs to be
validated on an independent sample of subjects, as was done by Nuttall et al. (1977) in the context of
the Home Office's Score. Often the luxury of a second sample will not be possible, in which case a
recently developed statistical theory of shrinkage can be used to assess the likely stability of risk
scores (Copas, 1983; 1993).

Table 1.

		increment
Age at offence:	under21	+5
	21 to 24	+1
	25 to 39	0
	40 to 49	-1
	50 and over	-2
Number of associates:	3 or fewer	0
	4 or more	+4

Just as there are hard and soft interpretations of a statistical predictor, there is a similar division
between methods of constructing prediction scores. The Burgess method is a "soft" method since it is
not based on any particular probability model. Logistic regression and shrinkage theory, together
with almost all other mainstream statistical techniques, are "hard" methods since they involve specific
probability models, usually parametric models specifying how the probability of reoffending is related
to the various indicator factors. It is obvious, however, that a score constructed by a hard method still
defines risk groups and so can be given the soft interpretation which this paper is advocating. The
fact that the best predictors, when judged by the soft interpretation, seem to rely on hard methods for
their construction, is a matter of some subtlety.

Survival curves and prediction scores

The statistical prediction scales envisaged so far have related to offending or reconviction within a
fixed time period, often taken as two years. For decision-making in parole, however, the period of
interest should be related to the length of potential parole that may be granted. This is made explicit
in the new Criminal Justice Act, which poses an interesting statistical problem when it requires that
"the parole decision should be based upon an evaluation of the risk to the public of the person
committing a further serious offence at a time when he would otherwise be in prison". Under the recent
legislation, the period for potential parole extends from one half to two thirds of the way through the
sentence. Parole is only envisaged for sentences of four years or more, so the parole period can range
from a minimum of eight months to a maximum of two years or more for very long sentences.
Shorter periods may also be involved if parole is deferred and reconsidered at a later date. The
requirement, therefore, is for a prediction score which can be adjusted for different exposure times.

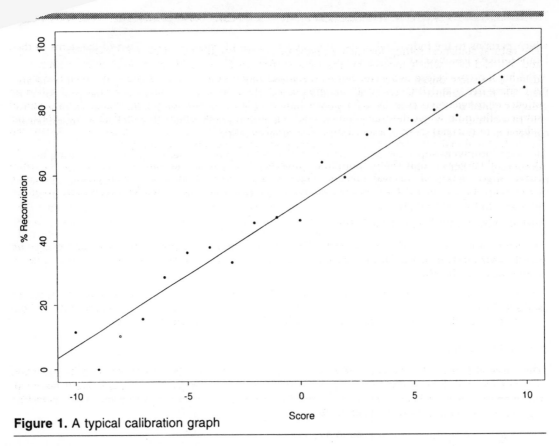

Figure 1. A typical calibration graph

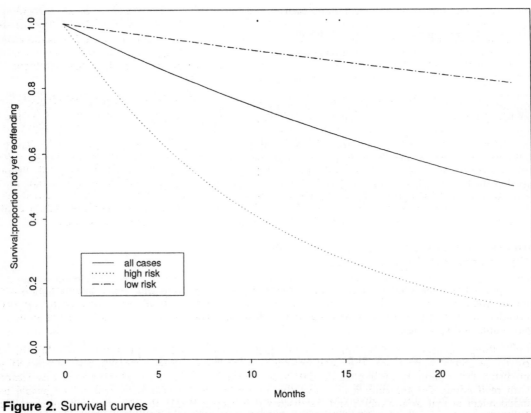

Figure 2. Survival curves

The natural statistical setting for such a predictor is survival analysis (Cox and Oakes, 1984; ∿ and Witte, 1988), which focuses on the time of first reoffence or reconviction, rather than sim₊ whether it occurs before two years. Survival analysis models the time of transition between two states, A ("crime-free") and B ("recidivist"). Every subject starts in state A and moves to state B when an offence or conviction occurs. Data for survival analysis take the form of noting, for each of a cohort of subjects, the time when the transition occurs, and if none is observed, the total time for which the subject's record has been followed up. A statistical predictor needs to assess the risk that an individual will make the transition before some given length of time (e.g. one year).

A survival curve is simply the proportion of subjects who, by time t, are still in state A. Figure 2 (solid curve) shows a typical survival curve for (known) reoffending after release from prison. The curve necessarily starts at one at $t = 0$ and decreases as t increases. The risk of reoffending within any given time period t is now simply:

Risk for time t = 1 – Survival curve at t

As before, a statistical predictor uses indicator factors to define risk groups, but now each risk group has its own survival curve. Each risk group needs to be calibrated in terms of its survival curve, rather than a single reoffending rate.

There is no simple analogue of the Burgess method for survival curves, and rather more complicated statistical techniques are needed. The basic idea is to posit some underlying offending rate λ, from which it can be shown that the survival curve takes the precise mathematical form:

Survival curve at $t = e^{-\lambda}$

The curve is indexed by the value of λ, small λ giving a shallow curve (reoffending only occurring infrequently) and large λ giving a steep curve (frequent reoffending). If this formulation is accepted, the quantity λ is the label for risk groups, and the standard procedure for survival analysis is to fit a log-linear model for λ (Dobson, 1990) by which:

$\log \lambda = a_0 + a_1 \times age + a_2 \times no.\ of\ previous\ convictions\ + ...,$

this weighted sum extending over those factors which are believed to be indicative of reoffending. Computer software is available for estimating the weights $a_0, a_2 ...$ (Aitkin et al., 1989). Once these weights are determined, any given set of values of the factors converts into the score λ; this identifies the risk group in which the individual belongs, the above formula then specifies the survival curve, and hence the predicted risk score for any time t of interest. The dotted and dashed curves in Figure 2 show typical survival curves for two contrasting risk groups.

Although this formulation illustrates the principles of survival analysis, and may be adequate for practical purposes, some modifications are usually needed to ensure that the survival curve for each risk group corresponds closely to the previously observed pattern of offending. The assumption that the value of λ for each risk group remains constant is a reasonable approximation for short time periods, but a useful generalization is to allow λ to vary with time. This can be accomplished by fitting so-called Weibull survival curves, as explained in Aitkin et al. (1989). Another useful generalization is to use a "split-population model" such as Broadhurst and Mallor (1991). The idea here is to restrict the survival model to just part of the population of subjects, it being assumed that the remainder will never reoffend. Although not mentioned explicitly in the book by Aitkin et al. (1989), these models can also be fitted using the package GLIM on which the book is based.

Some methodological issues

This paper has considered some statistical aspects of prediction scores and their interpretation. Much more research remains to be done on how to develop good statistical predictors. There are also broader methodological issues that need to be addressed. The paper concludes by listing some of these outstanding issues.

(a) Nothing has been said about the choice of which factors to use in the prediction score, but this is clearly of crucial importance. The usual procedure is to obtain data on a large number of potentially predictive factors, and then to explore the data to see which factors are statistically significantly associated with reoffending. The difficulty here is that the information in any one factor will not in general be independent of that in any other, and, as discussed in Copas (1985), the statistical significance of a factor is only indirectly related to its efficacy in prediction. A compromise is usually needed between statistical and practical considerations - only a predictor which involves a relatively small number of factors, and which is seen to be intuitively sensible is likely to be accepted and used in practice.

(b) No satisfactory method seems to be available for measuring the quality of a statistical predictor. The usual procedure is to calculate the "percentage correctly classified" mentioned in Section 2, but this is based on an artificial "decision" based on an arbitrary threshold, and does not measure the specificity of the risk groups or the accuracy with which the score has been calibrated against observed reoffending. A measure is needed by which to compare prediction scales in different applications, or for different data on which predictors might be considered, or for different sample sizes.

(c) A dictum for experimentation in scientific research is "if you want to know what happens when you change the system, you have to change it". Obviously the scope for experimentation in criminology is limited or non-existent. But for parole the system has changed quite radically under the new Criminal Justice Act, and yet a statistical predictor to suit the new arrangements can only be based on data relating to cases before the change. Some guidance might be given by comparing the reoffending rates of those paroled, in the past, and seeing how much of the difference is explained by differences in the predictive factors, but inevitably some faith is needed in the robustness of predictors to changes in the administrative system. Grounds for such faith can be found in Ward (1987) who showed that the Home Office's present parole predictor remained fairly stable from before to after the introduction of parole in England and Wales.

A broader aspect of the same point is that a prediction score describes statistical associations observed in the past, and cannot be given a direct causal interpretation. Suppose, for example, that data from a broad spectrum of offenders are studied, some of whom are given prison sentences, some of whom are given non-custodial sentences. It will typically be found that reoffending rates after sentence will be lower for the prison sample than for the non-custodial sample. This is partially, but not wholly, explained by the differences in a typical set of predictive factors. To deduce from this that to change the penalties for particular individuals to custodial rather than non-custodial sentences will result in a decrease in the rate of reoffending is clearly invalid. More generally, caution is needed when a predictor is used in a context different from that envisaged when it was constructed.

Predictors have sometimes been constructed using data on reconvictions, and yet used as if they relate to reoffending. Only a proportion of reoffences, even if they are actually committed, result in conviction, and the problem of under-reporting is an ever-present one. Reporting rates certainly depend on crime type relating to previous convictions as predictive factors in the score, to the extent that there is some evidence of crime specialization. When a prediction score is based on survival analysis of dates of first (known) reoffences, it is necessary to allow for the delay between offence and conviction. This is another cause of under-reporting of offences occurring near the end of the follow-up period. Some statistical adjustments are possible to allow for this, but the safest solution is to ensure that follow-up extends sufficiently beyond the period for which prediction is required, curtailing the scope of the survival analysis if necessary. As much as a year's extra follow-up will usually be needed to capture nearly all of the reoffence dates.

References

AITKIN, M., ANDERSON, D., FRANCES, B., and HINDE, J. (1989) **Statistical Modelling in GLIM.** Oxford: Clarendon Press

BROADHURST, R. G., and MALLOR, R. A. (1991) Estimating the numbers of prison terms in criminal careers from one-step probabilities of recidivism. **Journal of Quantitative Criminology, 7,** 275-290

BURGESS, E. W. (1928) Factors determining success or failure on parole. In A. A. Bruce, A. J. Harno, E. W. Burgess and J. Landesco (Eds) **The Workings of the Intermediate-sentence Law and the Parole System in Illinois.** Springfield: Illinois State Board of Parole

COLLETT, D. (1991) **Modelling Binary Data.** London: Chapman & Hall

COPAS, J. B. (1983) Regression, prediction and shrinkage (with discussion). **Journal of the Royal Statistical Society, B, 45,** 311-354

COPAS, J. B. (1985) Prediction equations, statistical analysis and shrinkage. In D. P. Farrington and R. Tarling (Eds) **Prediction in Criminology.** Albany: State University of New York Press

COPAS, J. B. (1993) The shrinkage of point scoring methods. **Applied Statistics, 42,** 315-331

COPAS, J. B., and WHITELEY, S. (1976) Predicting success in the treatment of psychopaths. **British Journal of Psychiatry, 129,** 388-392

COX, D. R., and OAKES, D. (1984) **Analysis of Survival Data.** London: Chapman & Hall

DOBSON, J. J. (1990) **An Introduction to Generalized Linear Models** (second edition). London: Chapman & Hall

FITZMAURICE, C., BIDDLE, F., and STANBY, P. (1991) **SPS: Sentence Prediction Scale.** Research Report, Staffordshire Probations Service

HUMPHREY, C., CARTER, P., and PEASE, K. (1991) **A Reconviction Predictor for Probationers.** Research Report, Department of Accounting and Social Policy, University of Manchester

MANHEIM, H., and WILKENS, L. T. (1955) **Prediction Methods in Relation to Borstal Training.** London: HMSO

MERRINGTON, S. (1990) **The Cambridgeshire Risk of Reconviction Scale.** Research Report, Cambridgeshire Probation Service

NUTTALL, C. P., et al. (1977) Parole in England and Wales. **Home Office Research Study, 38.** London: HMSO

SCHMIDT, P., and WITTE, A. D. (1988) **Predicting Recidivism Using Survival Models.** New York: Springer-Verlag

WARD, W. (1987) **The Validity of the Reconviction Prediction Score.** Home Office Research Study 94. London: HMSO

Dissociative identity disorder and self-injury: a review of the literature and case history

Anne Carpenter and Juliana C. MacLeod

Following on from Julie MacLeod's clinical presentation of a client presenting with Dissociative Identity Disorder (DID) and Self-injurious Behaviour, there is a literature review on DID. DID is the new DSMIV category for what has been called Multiple Personality Disorder. DID has been viewed with some scepticism but several clinical psychologists have found increasing presentation of such disorders in survivors of sexual abuse. The literature review considers the contentious issues of diagnosis, treatment and criminal responsibility. In addition, some consideration is given to the possible aetiology of the disorder and it is suggested that dissociation is a coping mechanism developed in childhood and can be seen to some degree in many abuse survivors.

Multiple Personality Disorder, or Dissociative Identity Disorder as it is to be named in DSM-IV, has been a controversial diagnosis for decades and until the last ten years seemed to have been largely abandoned. However, with the increasing number of adult sexual abuse survivors being seen by therapists, predominantly in the USA and Canada, there has been a growing interest in the disorder which has been reflected in a growth in research and literature. In this paper we hope to air some of the issues in Dissociative Identity Disorder (DID) and present a case of a woman with self-mutilating behaviour.

The area of DID is particularly relevant in the forensic field because of the issues of diagnosis and criminal responsibility. This case study is also of interest as self-mutilating behaviour is unfortunately common in female prison populations and similarities may exist.

What is DID?

In the late nineteenth century, psychologists such as Pierre Janet and Morton Prince discussed the disorder but until the last decade the dominant belief was that the syndrome was "an artefact, a dramatic fantasy enacted by highly hypnotizable patients with a covert or overt encouragement of the therapist". Over history there have been frequent references to devil possession and out of body experiences, but when Freud repudiated the seduction theory and therapists did not accept the validity of sexual abuse disclosures, many feel that DID became even more unacceptable as a diagnosis. The link between the history of prolonged and severe child sexual abuse and Dissociative Identity Disorder is seen in 90 per cent of the cases. The DSMIII-R criteria for Multiple Personality Disorder are:

(a) the existence with the person of two or more distinct personalities or personality states (each with its own relatively enduring pattern of perceiving, relating to and thinking about the environment and self).

(b) At least two of these personality states recurrently take full control of the person's behaviour.

The clinical manifestations of such a syndrome are as follows:

1. An intense and chronic form of Post Traumatic Stress Disorder.

2. A coping mechanism developed in childhood as a response to severe and prolonged abuse.

3. Sudden and unexplainable shifts in personality.

4. Dense amnesia for events which occur when other personalities prevail.

5. Splits may have different names, ages and genders. These splits are essentially exaggerated parts of the self that have been fragmented by severe and repeated environmental stress.

If we take a profile of a normal personality the bar chart represents the normal personality. Each normal and complete personality has different facets to it. There may be times at which the person relates to colleagues in a work situation in a particular fashion. Equally they may relate to their family in a different fashion. They may have memories of childhood contained within one part of the personality and particular feelings or impulses contained in another part. Essentially the complete personality is able to move within the different moods amid different memories with relative ease. The person is also fully aware of the different facets of themselves.

With a split personality or Dissociative Identity Disorder, people commonly refer to the splits as personalities, implying a complete personality with a range of characteristics. In our opinion while the splits may differ in age, name and gender, rather than being whole, they are exaggerated parts of the complete self that have been fragmented by severe repeated emotional stress. These splits serve separate and important functions. They may contain forbidden feelings, impulses or memories that are so difficult for the person to face that they split off and develop a "life" of their own.

These splits are essentially fragmented parts of the self that serve the function of expressing feelings, impulses and behavioural memories. Fike (1990) described the various splits that may present in a personality:

Primary personality
This split tends to present as dependent, over eager to please. It is a legal entity and often presents as bland and emotionless.

Child or adolescent split
This part often has to endure the abuse and may present as a frightened child or children. There may be several if the need to split continued as the abuse continued and presented more conflicts for the child.

Protective splits
These may save the others from intolerable conditions, for example, by fighting or fleeing.

Negative or hostile splits
This is often apparently an internalized image of the abuser and may be relieved by cutting and burning. This is of particular interest in terms of self-mutilating behaviour.

Perpetrator splits
This part of the personality may be forced to abuse others and retains memories of such perpetrations of abuse. They may also continue to be actively involved in abuse and this is obviously of particular interest in the area of forensic psychology. Stress precipitates the transitions between splits and can be dramatic, for example, falling asleep or fainting or can be subtle, for example, changes in facial expression, posture or non-verbal behaviour.

Aetiology

How does this particular state develop? DID would appear to be a coping mechanism representing an extreme form of normal coping mechanisms. We all can dissociate to a certain extent, for example, by forgetting putting something in a particular place or forgetting part of a journey. It can also be used to cope with trauma or when concentration is taken up by another activity.

Children are known to have a good imagination and engage readily in pretend play calling themselves by different names and having imaginary companions. If children are continually being presented with inconsistencies and have painful and confusing experiences inflicted on them, dissociating into a fantasy world allows them a form of coping. If such conflicting messages and abuse continue it becomes a habit which leads to additional problems in childhood. It is this maladaptive coping response that must be treated.

Kluft (1984) listed the following as aetiology of Multiple Personality Disorder:

1. Patients with Multiple Personality Disorder are extremely good at dissociation.

2. Patients with Multiple Personality Disorder have used dissociation to cope with severe childhood trauma.

3. The form and structure of MPD varied depending on the person's temperament and non-abusive experience.

4. The abuse did not stop and the victim did not receive enough love and care to heal her wounds.

The treatment of DID

Treatment essentially follows the guidelines of working with any survivor of child sexual abuse. In addition the following are essential:

1. To establish trust.

2. Establish contact with splits.

3. Share the diagnosis in a gentle and non-suggestive way.

4. Help the original personality to acknowledge and work through memories, emotions and impulses that are expressed by others.

5. Fusion and integration of the splits.

6. Hospital treatment when necessary.

The question must remain as to why mental health professionals are so divided on the issue of Multiple Personality Disorder.

Bruce-Jones and Coid (1992) felt that the rise in cases presenting with Multiple Personality Disorder was a factor of its inclusion in the DSMIII categories. They argue therefore that it should not be included in ICD9, otherwise there may be an equivalent rise in cases in the UK.

The issue of diagnosis is fundamental. Many argue that the disorder meets the criteria for borderline personality disorder and it is often impossible to differentiate the two. Diagnosis is often difficult for the following reasons.

There is a subtle presentation of symptoms and the patient may be afraid of divulging information for fear of disbelief or that they may be considered mad. There are periods of non-dissociation which may confuse the diagnosis and personality changes may be attributed to normal mood changes. It has been suggested that therapists may be reluctant to believe stories of abuse and that this may lead to a shortfall in diagnoses. The syndrome is essentially unpredictable, polymorphous and asteriotypic in appearance and the presence of other psychiatric conditions or symptoms of other disorders may also confuse the diagnosis. Putnam (1986) found that there was a core of depressive and dissociative symptoms in people presenting with Multiple Personality Disorder. Ninety per cent of those presenting reported depressive symptoms, 70 per cent had mood swings and 95 per cent of those had one or more psychiatric diagnoses. It had also been noted that many present with psychopathic features and this may be accounted for by flatness of affect in reporting many traumatic experiences and often a very chaotic lifestyle will be seen in people presenting with DID. In addition, Kluft (1985) identified some Schneiderian first ranked symptoms in patients with DID and this may lead to them being diagnosed as schizophrenic. The fact that many of the people presenting with DID have had multiple previous psychiatric contacts and diagnoses may also make clinicians reluctant to find a diagnosis of DID or Multiple Personality Disorder.

The question of diagnosis is clearly most important in the area of forensic psychology and psychiatry and its bearing on criminal responsibility and fitness to plead. This has been an area which has caused considerable discussion in the area of research in DID and together theorists have reached a common ground on the area of criminal responsibility.

Kenneth Bianci, "the Hillside Strangler", is perhaps the most important case of someone faking MPD in an effort to avoid the death penalty. He was successful in his faking. Peer (1991) cites the case of Mr A and Billy Rae who was charged with sadistic murder. He gave a defence of not guilty by reason of insanity. His defence was:

Because of the nature of (MPD), the host personality is not able to fully know right from wrong and even to "know" the nature and quality of the act (of murder).

... A does not meet the standards required of criminal responsibility.

(This plea turned out to be successful and Peer notes that the patient's behaviour, while in a psychiatric institution, reinforced the diagnosis of MPD or DID.)

He goes on to mention another case of a woman who was charged with driving while under the influence of alcohol. She claims that her alter had been present and had been responsible for her drinking and driving. Her defence was that she had no recollection of the act and therefore could not answer questions related to it. The court did not accept the plea and stated that whatever personality had awareness, that person would still be responsible for the act.

Ross (1989) sums up the opinion on the use of MPD as a defence.

Using MPD (as a defence) ... does not teach patients how to take ownership of their lives or responsibility for their actions.

It is essential, especially when working with severely disturbed multiples who are prone to theatrical, manipulative and double-binding behaviour, to insist that the patient is responsible for the behaviour of all alters.

The opinion therefore on the use of DID and MPD as a plea for limited responsibility in criminal acts is that the personality is still equally responsible for the behaviour and suffering from a dissociative disorder does not constitute a lack of fitness to plead.

References

BRUCE-JONES, W., and COID, J. (1992) Identity diffusion presenting as multiple personality disorder in a female psychopath. **British Journal of Psychiatry, 160,** 541-544

COONS, P. M. (1986) Child abuse and Multiple Personality Disorder: review of the literature and suggestions for treatment. **Child Abuse and Neglect, 16,** 455-462

FIKE, M. L. (1990) Clinical manifestations in persons with Multiple Personality Disorder. **American Journal of Occupational Therapy, 44,** ii, 984-990

MERSKEY, H. (1992) The manufacture of personalities. the production of Multiple Personality Disorder. **British Journal of Psychiatry, 160,** 327-340

PERR, I. N. (1991) Crime and Multiple Personality Disorder: a case history and discussion. **Bulletin of the American Academy of Psychiatry Law, 19,** 203-214

ROSS, C. (1989) Multiple Personality Disorder. **Diagnosis, Clinical Features and Treatment.** John Wiley & Sons

Appendix

This report focuses on the self-injuring behaviours of a client suffering from Dissociative Identity Disorder. Details of the client's background have been omitted to ensure confidentiality.

Case A

A is a woman in her late thirties whose initial contact with the Psychiatric Services took place after an overdose of paracetamol. Early diagnoses varied and in the first year following initial contact A was variously described as "a manipulative personality" as her story kept changing, "a complex mix of psychiatric and personality problems" and "hysterical". Amongst other symptoms she exhibited memory loss, child-like behaviours, regressions, vacant spells and agitation. Self-injuries included burning, biting, cutting and overdoses. A's contact with the Clinical Psychology Services began a year later after another hospital admission following an overdose of 20 to 30 paracetamol.

At assessment, A reported frequent sexual abuse by a number of abusers from the age of 5 until 18. At times she had clear memories of the abuse and on other occasions felt as if she had imagined everything. She could find herself in a place without knowing how she got there and sometimes did not recognize friends, relatives or neighbours. She experienced flashbacks, regressions and severe mood swings and was very frightened by her symptoms. During sessions her voice and expression would suddenly change and she would discuss events from her childhood and teenage years as if they were happening in the present. Initially these changes were accompanied by a great deal of agitation and distress. Attempts to orientate the client to the present simply led to confusion and further distress. At times A could see a man on the wall of the interview room; he seemed very real and frightening and she felt that he would punish her for talking to me.

Test results

A had a dissociation score of 66 on the Dissociation Scale (Bernstein and Putnam, 1986) and had significant scores on the anxiety, conversion, depression, ruminative and dissociative sub-scales of the Diagnostic Signs and Symptoms Inventory (Foulds and Bedford, 1978).

Self-injuries

A injured herself in a variety of different ways:

(a) by scratching until bleeding;

(b) burning her arms and abdomen;

(c) cutting various parts of the body (she would identify and hide sharp objects to use when needed);

(d) repeated overdoses: A would hide paracetamol whenever possible and took three overdoses in the month preceding initial contact with Clinical Psychology Services. She had no idea as to why she hurt herself but felt that it reduced the tension. She usually only became aware of an injury after it had happened and had no memory of having done it herself. She did not appear to feel any pain, even when the injury was severe.

A was asked to keep a chart to get further details of her injuries. She was asked to record the following: day, date, time; type of injury; what you were doing before the injury; how you feel; what you were thinking; and were you aware of carrying out the injury.

While these charts provided detailed information about the frequency and type of injury, A rarely knew what she was feeling or thinking at the time. The injury was usually brought to her attention by someone else.

Initially, scratching had the highest frequency, although this ceased after the sixth week: biting ceased after week three. A took a mild overdose in week six and week sixteen. Burning occurred infrequently after week two. Cutting was the most common form of injury until week 25 when no self-harming behaviours occurred.

It was also suggested that *A* keep a diary to try and identify any precipitating factors. She was encouraged to write whenever she wished to do so and was given no instructions as to what to write. *A* wrote in her diary on a daily basis. The handwriting in the diary varied considerably from a mature script to child-like print with poor spelling and grammar. This change in writing often took place in the middle of a sentence. *A* refused to read what she had written. Any attempt to read it to her led to severe agitation and often triggered the emergence of a younger self. Unlike the charts, the diary was very informative both in terms of identifying triggers for the injury and providing details of the childhood abuse and the feelings that this created.

The adult *A* feels the urge to harm herself although she does not know why and battles against it. Her writing changes as she identifies a crying patient as the cause of her distress, which appears to trigger memories of her abuser. She writes about her fear of being hurt by her abuser if she cries and that she would like to go to heaven so that her abuser will not find her. At the end of the extract the adult *A* feels suicidal. This feeling persists throughout the next day although *A* doesn't know why she is feeling this way.

A's self-injury does not make sense unless it is analysed using data from the diary which indicates that various triggers cause *A* to regress to times in her childhood when she was being abused.

In fact, the abuse can be seen as "logical" if it is understood from the viewpoint of a child trying to cope with trauma. For example, self-injury can be seen as a way of alerting other adults to the abuse. It can give the child a sense of control ("if I cut myself maybe the abuser won't have to") or a sense of power ("the abuser will see the cuts and be afraid that the abuse will be discovered and so leave me alone"). One of the common results of childhood sexual abuse is a feeling of being dirty and some self-injury can be seen as a way of becoming clean, for example, "if I bleed all of the dirt will come out and I will be clean".

A's diary also provided data about day-to-day triggers for traumatic memories. For example, a crying child reminded her of the child that she lost when she had an abortion in her teens.

Treatment of self-harming behaviour

The adult *A* was very keen to stop harming herself and her diary reveals a regular battle between the urge to harm herself and her sense that it was not doing her any good. Discussion of the injury usually led to the emergence of the alter responsible and the following approach was taken.

(a) allow the alter to discuss the issue triggering the injury (usually relating to the abuser or abusers); reassure the alter that she was now safe; help the alter clarify what she hoped to achieve by hurting herself, and provide alternative coping mechanisms for reaching this goal.

(b) the adult *A* was also encouraged to talk to staff when agitated rather than retreating to her room alone.

Table 3 shows the reduction in frequency of self-harm during the first 25 weeks of treatment.

There was a large decrease in depression and ruminative scores and *A* no longer endorsed items concerning self-harm. There was also a small decrease in dissociative scores. Scores on the conversion, obsessional and phobic sub-scales increased the latter by three points. These were related to *A*'s reluctance to go out alone for fear of meeting her abuser.

Summary

When dealing with a patient suffering from a dissociative disordered illness, it must be remembered that self-injuring may appear illogical when viewed in the context of an adult's current circumstances. For example, *A*'s use of self-harming behaviours as a way of reducing tension did not make sense either to herself or to the staff providing care. Her self-injury only makes sense if viewed in the context of early childhood abuse and a child's attempt to deal with the consequence of the abuse and to control the environment. In the case of *A*, dealing with these issues has led to a significant reduction in self-injury and in her overall symptom levels.

Note: September 1994

A is currently living in sheltered accommodation and plans are being made for her to return to completely independent living in the near future. She self-injured on six further occasions between week 25 and week 35. No self-injury has taken place in the last 12 weeks.

Psychological Models in Criminal Justice

Arising from the multidisciplinary workshops held in Oxford in January and April on "Psychological Models in Criminal Justice", members of the Group formed then (which now meets regularly) were invited to take part in the above Symposium at Newbold Revel. Three papers (by Blackburn, Boyle and Fulford) are published here. The first paper was given by Bill Fulford, Research Fellow in Philosophy at Green College, Oxford and Honorary Consultant Psychiatrist at the Warneford Hospital. Dr Fulford spoke extempore and was unable to prepare a paper in time for the present publication. He has, however, authorized the following account made from the abstract of his talk, notes taken by the Convenor on that occasion and at the Mental Health Act Conference held in November 1993, and from the "position paper" offered by Dr Fulford before the January workshop.

Charmian Bollinger
Convenor

Cognitive functioning or practical reasoning? Two models of delusion as disease

William Fulford

The concept of irrationality underpins a number of important ethical and medicolegal aspects of psychiatric practice, including the status of mental illness as an excuse in law and involuntary psychiatric treatment. The standard account of rationality in the bioethical literature is based on the presence of specific competencies. This is consistent with the irrationality shown by some forms of mental illness – for example, dementia. It is also consistent with the standard "medical model" of mental illness, according to which it is to be understood in terms of disturbances of mental functioning. However, a study of the phenomenology of delusion carried out by the author (see Moral Theory and Medical Practice, 1990) showed that the standard account wholly fails to explain the irrationality shown by other forms of mental illness, in particular, the forensically significant functional psychotic disorders such as schizophrenia, hypomania and psychotic depression. In addition to specific competencies, irrationality may involve a disturbance of Aristotelian practical reasoning. This conclusion connects forensic psychiatry with work in the philosophy of mind on the structure of action and intentionality.

Orientation

Although well established in criminal law, the insanity defence and related questions of legal capacity remain highly problematic in practice. This is due in part to the obscurity of both legal and medical notions of rationality. The medical concept of irrationality underpins a number of important ethical and medicolegal aspects of psychiatric practice, including the status of mental illness as an excuse in law, and criteria for involuntary psychiatric treatment.

In discussions of these issues, a "medical" model of mental illness is generally adopted in which it is treated merely as an extension of physical illness. Mental illness is assumed to be a value-free notion defined by reference to objective norms of disturbed functioning.

It is argued that this approach fails to do justice to the remarkable diversity of mental disorders and, in particular, is inconsistent with the clinical features of the forensically central symptom of delusion.

An alternative to the standard medical model is outlined, the main features of which are (i) a recognition of the importance of value judgments in the diagnosis of mental disorders and (ii) an emphasis on the significance of failure of action (or incapacity) in the actual experience of illness, physical as well as mental.

This "value-based" model helps to explain the variety of mental disorders and is consistent with the phenomenology of delusions. It also suggests an account of both medical and legal concepts of insanity. A framework is thus provided for future work, empirical as well as conceptual, directed towards clarifying the grounds of the insanity defence. Some of the conflicts between the centrality of value judgments in this account and the traditional role of the psychiatrist as an expert to the facts are indicated.

Using linguistic analysis, that is, observing how words are actually used, rather than using dictionary definitions, it becomes clear that discussions of "illness" involve value judgments as well as descriptive statements.

The present account starts from a series of case vignettes which together contribute to a conceptual map of the field of psychiatry.

Delusion - standard account

The standard account of rationality in the bioethical literature is based on the presence of specific competencies. This is consistent with the irrationality shown in some forms of mental illness, for example, dementia. However, a study of the phenomenology of delusion carried out by the present author (Fulford, 1990) showed that the standard account wholly fails to explain the irrationality shown by other forms, in particular the forensically significant functional psychotic disorders, such as schizophrenia, hypomania and psychotic depression.

The "medical model" of delusions equates the disease that they imply with failures, or disturbances, of mental functioning. This is to omit from consideration the person's own experience of illness and the failure of action which can be seen as a failure of Aristotelian "practical reasoning", that is, the reasons people give for what they do.

What is it that defines a delusion? Does the belief need to be false?

Cases

Case (i) Mr A.B., a bank manager, aged 48, presented with head and facial pains. There were clinical features of depression, biological symptoms and a history which included a previous suicide attempt. His "delusion" was a hypochondriacal one - he believed he had "advanced brain cancer". Since it was established that he did not have brain cancer, the delusion is objectively false.

Case (ii) Mr A., aged 50, was a dustman. He was diagnosed as suffering from pathological jealousy, convinced that his wife was having an affair. In fact, his wife had had an affair and was currently depressed because it had broken up.

Was he, or was he not, deluded?

Case (iii) is a paradoxical one, in which the patient's central delusion was that he was "mentally ill" and it was this fear which led to his being diagnosed as "deluded" (and thus mentally ill!).

It seems that delusions do not have to be, objectively, false.

Delusion - alternative account

It has been suggested that insanity involves a disturbance of cognitive functioning, but there is no evidence, from a number of studies, that this is the case. An alternative view examines the person's experience and the failure of action.

Case (iv) Mr H., aged 32, made an unduly negative evaluation of events. He had - in reality - failed to give his children their pocket money. This led him to describe himself as "deeply wicked". His failure was a "sign of [his] worthlessness as a father" and "the family would be better off if [he] were dead".

Case (v) Miss G.F. made an unduly positive evaluation. Her bizarre behaviour could be explained by the fact that she thought she was Mary Magdalene and that the poetry she wrote was extremely great and profound.

Facts and values

It seems that delusions can take two main forms - they can occur as facts or as values. The facts can be true or false and the values can be negative or positive. In between these two, there is the paradoxical delusion, as in case (iii) above. It is this range of phenomena which leads to the account of delusions in terms of failure of practical reasoning.

Conclusions

In philosophy, facts and values are normally held to be like chalk and cheese. However, if we move away from thinking about cognitive dysfunction to consideration of disturbances of practical reasoning, then those reasons can involve both facts and values. What deluded people share is a distortion of the reasons they give for their behaviour. Whatever discoveries there may be in the physical sciences and in medicine, the patient's experience must thus remain central. This conclusion connects forensic psychiatry with work in the philosophy of mind on the structure of action and intentionality.

References

FULFORD, K.M.W. (1990) **Moral Theory and Medical Practice**. New York: Cambridge University Press

FULFORD, K.M.W. (1993) Value, action, mental illness, and the law. In S. Shute, J. Gardner and J. Horder (Eds) **Action and Value in Criminal Law**. Oxford: Oxford University Press.

Prescription and description, rationality and irrationality in the criminal justice system

Mary Boyle

This paper takes as its starting point two dimensions or sets of ideas which are fundamental to the operation of the criminal justice system, i.e. prescription/description and rationality/irrationality. The paper describes how these ideas operate within the system, how they are related, why they might have assumed such importance and why they are so problematic. Finally, it is suggested that in a system where the balance was more towards description than in the present system, then the dimension of rationality/irrationality might also come to assume less importance.

The subject matter of the criminal justice system is, of course, the law; but it is also human behaviour. The system seeks explanations for offending and attempts to predict what behaviour might be expected from offenders in the future. Inevitably, this involves the use, implicitly or explicitly, of models of behaviour, of assumptions as to why people behave as they do and about what is most likely to determine their future conduct. One of the more explicit aspects of the criminal justice system's models of behaviour is that of rationality: humans are presumed usually to behave in a rational way, to make free and deliberate choices and to understand the implications of these. People may, however, be deprived of reason temporarily or permanently and in this state may be incapable of exercising choice or of understanding the implications of their actions. It is this model of behaviour which underlies one of the most important distinctions made by the criminal justice system: that between offenders who are mentally normal (possessed of reason) and mentally abnormal (deprived of reason). This distinction was challenged by the British Psychological Society's 1973 submission to the Butler Committee on the Law Relating to the Mentally Abnormal Offender. This submission criticized the concept of "mental disease" and suggested the adoption of a developmental model of behaviour, which emphasized the development and learning of social and antisocial behaviour. Similarly, Blackman (1981) described a model of behaviour based on applied behavioural analysis which might encompass both "rational" and "irrational" offending behaviour. More recent criticisms have been provided by Bollinger (1993; 1994). The BPS submission was made at a time of considerable optimism over the potential of psychology to provide comprehensive analyses of behaviour and, more important, a technology for changing it. Although this optimism may have somewhat dimmed, particularly in terms of behaviour change, the concern with the criminal justice system's model of humans as rational and its implications for what happens to offenders remains as valid today as it was 20 years ago. In this paper, I want to examine further the problematic status of "rationality" in the criminal justice system and to relate it to a second set of ideas which are central to the system: that of prescription and description.

To take the second set first: the criminal justice system is self-evidently prescriptive - the very term "justice" implies this. The system contains a number of oughts: what ought to happen to people who behave in certain ways, that the punishment ought to fit the crime, and so on. Of course, as psychologists, we have nothing special to contribute to what ought to happen to people who break the law although we can take a keen interest in how ideas about what ought to happen to law-breakers are socially constructed and in how such ideas operate in practice. But the justice system is also descriptive in the sense that it is expected, however implicitly, that what is thought to be punishment will deter offenders from reoffending and will deter the rest of us from offending at all. It is when these two elements clash or contradict each other, as they frequently do, that problems arise. For example, psychologists define punishment as any consequence which reduces the likelihood of recurrence of the behaviour preceding it, and emphasize that what constitutes punishment must be determined empirically. There are, however, strongly held popular beliefs about what constitutes proper punishment and about what ought to happen to people who behave in certain ways, regardless of the outcome. As a result, consequences which might increase the likelihood of reoffending are considered to be proper punishment, while consequences which might decrease offending may be proscribed because they do not match lay ideas about punishment.

This clash between prescription and description, and its relationship to "rationality" become particularly problematic when we consider them in relation to so-called mentally abnormal offenders. A wide variety of language is used in talking about this group of offenders: defect of reason, diminished responsibility, unintentional acts, disease of the mind, insanity, irresistible impulse, not capable of understanding the difference between right and wrong or of understanding the nature and consequences of their behaviour, and so on. I shall not consider the whole range of circumstances which might lead to at least some of this language of unreason being invoked, but shall concentrate on those circumstances involving a diagnosis of what is said to be serious mental disorder. If such a diagnosis is applied, and particularly if any delusions or hallucinations relate specifically to a serious offence, then there is a good chance that the offender will be sent to a special hospital or secure unit rather than to an ordinary prison. We are so used to this aspect of the criminal justice system - that some people will be sent to hospital as a result of committing crimes - that perhaps we do not enquire closely enough about why this should be done. I would suggest that it is here, when we consider the possible reasons why we send some offenders to prison and others to hospital, that the ideas of prescription and description and rationality and irrationality become entangled in a particularly problematic way.

It has been suggested (Moran, 1985) that, historically, the features of the insanity defence, that is, the defence that the accused was in effect deprived of reason at the time of the crime, grew out of the dual desires to punish and to deter defendants judged to be mentally ill, and not out of a humanitarian concern for their welfare. Whether or not this was the case, it is, in fact, surprisingly difficult to find clear and explicit statements about why we continue to send some offenders to prison and others to hospital. There seem, however, to be two key ideas involved, even if these are implicit or only referred to in passing. The first is that it would be inhumane and therefore unjust to punish those who cannot be held responsible for their behaviour. Of course, this idea involves lay theories about punishment and it is ironic that some offenders should regard being confined in a special hospital as more aversive than being in prison (White, 1985; Poitier, 1993). The second assumption which seems to underlie this separation of offenders is that people said to be suffering from serious mental disorder would not be amenable to punishment because their behaviour is not under their control.

These two ideas clearly involve a mixture of prescription and description. They also involve a third assumption which is rarely made explicit and that is this: that "insane" behaviour is subject to a different set of determinants than is the behaviour of "sane" people. In other words that insane behaviour is not understandable in terms of theories which cover ordinary behaviour; because it is judged to be irrational, it is beyond our usual understanding. If we look at definitions of phenomena which are central to ideas of insanity, such as hallucinations and delusions, it is clear that the inability of an observer to identify ordinary social or personal factors which are controlling the behaviour or experience is crucial to the judgement that the person is seriously abnormal or is showing symptoms of an illness (see, e.g. Al-Issa, 1977; Oltmanns, 1988; Strauss, 1989).

These ideas are problematic for a number of reasons (see, for example, Boyle, 1990; 1992), not least because their validity is simply assumed; it has never been demonstrated. Given this, it seems likely that social and cultural factors must play an important role in the maintenance of these assumptions. Two factors seem to be particularly important here. The first is the remarkably high status which Western society accords the idea of reason or rationality. This status has, of course, been strongly reinforced by the dominance of science; it has also facilitated that dominance. But as Foucault (1965) has pointed out, it was precisely this lauding of rationality which allowed, or perhaps even required, the creation of a subclass said to be deficient in it. The second factor which seems to help maintain the idea of bizarre behaviour as irrationality is the pervasive and powerful medical model of behaviour we cannot understand. In a literal form, this model is central to the profession of psychiatry, although in a metaphorical form it also underlies much of clinical psychology theory. I have argued (Boyle, 1992) that the idea of madness as irrationality is indispensable to a literal medical model. It is so because, in the absence of direct evidence that the "mad" have anything wrong with their brains, the claim that their behaviour is not understandable provides grounds for assuming that the brain disorder is yet to be discovered. Indeed, it would be difficult to overestimate the threat to the literal medical model of madness, were we to abandon the notion that "mad" behaviour is in principle not understandable in relation to the culture in which it occurs. The literal medical model, however, also serves important functions for the general public, for relatives of those diagnosed as insane and for governments. One such function is to distract attention from social and cultural influences on bizarre behaviour and therefore apparently to absolve us of responsibility for it. It is also, of course, comforting to believe that those who behave in abhorrent ways are qualitatively different from the rest of us but can nevertheless be understood within a medical framework.

Yet if we look at the evidence, the idea of discontinuities between sanity and insanity, between reason and unreason, becomes very difficult to sustain. This evidence is only just beginning to accumulate, not least because the strength of the assumption that bizarre behaviour could not be understood in terms of ordinary theories was such as to deter many people from making the attempt. What evidence we do have about the "rationality" of bizarre behaviour comes from three sources. The first has been around for at least 25 years, particularly from learning theory approaches which demonstrated that the behaviour of people diagnosed as schizophrenic is extremely sensitive to environmental contingencies (Zarlock, 1966; Ayllon and Azrin, 1968). More recently, Falloon (1984) has provided an example of this process. In his work with "schizophrenics" and their families, he noted how difficult it was to change patients' antisocial behaviour within a medical framework, i.e. by assuming it to be related to their illness. Antisocial behaviour did decrease, however, when "normal" contingencies involving the police and the courts were put in place. This is not meant to suggest that arrest and incarceration is the answer for all offenders, but it does emphasize the problems of a priori assumptions that only some behaviours are influenced by environmental contingencies. The evidence that "mad" behaviour is very sensitive to environmental contexts is so strong that even those who support a literal medical model have accepted it. In order to retain the model, however, the non-specific concept of "vulnerability" has been posited, so that the environment exerts its effects on a biologically damaged person and produces an end-point state which remains beyond our understanding. Thus the distinction between rationality and irrationality can be preserved (see Johnson, 1993, for a critique of these approaches).

The second source of evidence that the sane/insane or rational/irrational distinction is problematic is the increasing body of evidence on the extent of "schizophrenic" behaviour, such as hallucinations and bizarre beliefs, in the general population. These phenomena have long been studied in other cultures by anthropologists or cross-cultural psychiatrists and psychologists (see, for example, Wallace, 1959; Al-Issa, 1977) but it is only relatively recently that bizarre behaviour and experiences amongst the non-psychiatric population, and their theoretical significance, have begun to be explored in Western cultures (Heise, 1988; Slade and Bentall, 1989). It is, arguably, the very high status accorded the idea of reason in Western cultures which has made us reluctant to confront our own irrationality or, indeed, to question the validity of such concepts when applied to human behaviour or experience.

The third source of evidence comes from qualitative research which attempts to make sense of bizarre behaviour by relating it to its interpersonal, social and cultural context. This work in fact attempts to understand behaviour which has been said in principle not to be understandable by the kind of theories we would apply to ourselves. Johnson (1989), for example, traces the development of bizarre beliefs in a young woman diagnosed as schizophrenic in relation to the woman's family background and the conflicting demands for dependence and autonomy. Similarly, Smith (1990) has provided a detailed analysis of the relationship between the behaviour and beliefs of Peter Sutcliffe (the "Yorkshire Ripper"), diagnosed as suffering from paranoid schizophrenia, and his personal and social background. Smith also argues that police investigations of Sutcliffe's crimes were significantly hampered by the conviction that the police were seeking a "mad" man who would be noticeably different from other men. Finally, Littlewood and Lipsedge (1989) have analysed the relationships between the bizarre behaviour and experiences and the social worlds of psychiatric patients from ethnic minorities, with a particular emphasis on the experience of racism and on conflicts between "old" and "new" cultures. What all of these analyses suggest is that rendering bizarre behaviour understandable requires at least four things. The first is a very detailed knowledge of the person's circumstances and the meanings which have been attached to them. The second is an acceptance of the central role of metaphor and personal, but none the less valid, meanings in speech. Third, we need to challenge psychology's and psychiatry's traditional neglect of the content of bizarre behaviour. Finally, we need to abandon the arrogant notion that our inability to understand someone's behaviour or experience makes these not understandable in principle, rather than that it reflects our ignorance or lack of imagination.

Where does this leave psychologists in relation to the criminal justice system? It certainly leaves us with a system laden with paradoxes and tensions where, for example, practices which are demonstrably ineffective or even harmful are retained because they satisfy the prescriptive element of the system;

where practices which may be helpful to those in prison can be frowned on because they do not seem sufficiently punitive; and where the consequences applied to those said not to deserve punishment may be much more aversive than those applied to ordinary prisoners. Such consequences may be tolerated because they involve the "treatment" of irrational people whose negative views on the treatment may be suspect. But the ideas which lie behind these aspects of the system have profound social and professional roots because they serve such important functions. It is these aspects of the system which may make it most resistant to change or to influence by empirical evidence. It is unlikely that the prescriptive aspect of the justice system could ever be dispensed with or that it would be desirable to do so. But the balance of the present system would appear to be too much in favour of prescription and of concepts and ideas which have little empirical support. What we could hope for is a system where the balance is shifted and where more descriptive questions are asked. If this were to happen, we might find that the rationality/irrationality distinction which underlies the separation of mentally "normal" and "abnormal" offenders would become less important. Instead, to a greater extent than now, we could ask descriptive questions about the social and personal antecedents of all offending behaviour and about what interventions - inevitably within certain social and moral constraints - might decrease the likelihood of reoffending.

References

AL-ISSA, I. (1977) Social and cultural aspects of hallucinations. **Psychological Bulletin, 84,** 570-587

AYLLON, T., and AZRIN, N. (1968) **The Token Economy: A motivational system for therapy and rehabilitation**. New York: Appleton Century Crofts

BLACKMAN, D. E. (1981) On the mental element in crime and behaviourism. In S. Lloyd-Bostock (Ed.) **Law and Psychology.** Oxford: SSRC Centre for Socio-legal Studies

BOLLINGER, C. (1993) The criminal justice system: a radical revision needed. **Clinical Psychology Forum, 59,** 31

BOLLINGER, C. (1994) Psychological models in criminal justice: conflict and challenge. **DCLP Newsletter, 37,** 29-33

BOYLE, M. (1990) **Schizophrenia: A scientific delusion?** London: Routledge.

BOYLE, M. (1992) Form and content, function and meaning in the analysis of schizophrenic behaviour. **Clinical Psychology Forum, 47,** 10-15

BRITISH PSYCHOLOGICAL SOCIETY (1973) Memorandum of evidence to the Butler Committee on the law relating to the mentally abnormal offender. **Bulletin of the British Psychological Society, 26,** 331-341

FOUCAULT, M. (1965) **Madness and Civilisation: A history of insanity in the age of reason.** New York: Pantheon

HEISE, D. R. (1988) Delusions and the construction of reality. In J. F. Oltmanns and B. A. Maher (Eds) **Delusional Beliefs.** New York: Wiley

JOHNSON, L. (1989) **Users and Abusers of Psychiatry**. London: Routledge

JOHNSON, L. (1993) Family management in "schizophrenia": its assumptions and contradictions. **Journal of Mental Health, 2,** 255-269

LITTLEWOOD, R., and LIPSEDGE, M. (1989) **Aliens and Alienists: Ethnic minorities and psychiatry** (second edition). London: Unwin Hyman

MORAN, R. (1985) The modern foundations for the insanity defence. **The Annals of the American Academy of Political and Social Science, 477,** 31-42

OLTMANNS, J. F. (1988) Approaches to the definition and study of delusions. In J. F. Oltmanns and B. A. Maher (Eds) **Delusional Beliefs.** New York: Wiley

POITIER, M. (1993) Giving evidence: women's lives in Ashworth Maximum Security Psychiatric Hospital. **Feminism and Psychology, 3**

SLADE, P. D., and BENTALL, R. P. (1988). **Sensory Deception: A scientific analysis of hallucinations.** London: Croom Helm

SMITH, J. (1990) **Misogynies.** London: Faber & Faber

STRAUSS, J. S. (1989) Subjective experience of schizophrenia: towards a new dynamic psychiatry. **Schizophrenia Bulletin, 15,** 179-187

WALLACE, A. F. C. (1959) Cultural determinants of response to hallucinatory experience. **Archives of General Psychiatry, 1,** 58-69

WHITE, S. (1985) The insanity defense in England and Wales since 1843. **The Annals of the American Academy of Political and Social Science, 477,** 43-57

ZARLOCK, S. P. (1966) Social expectations, language and schizophrenia. **Journal of Humanistic Psychology, 6,** 68-74

Psychopaths: are they bad or mad?

Ronald Blackburn

Definitions of psychopathic personality in terms of social deviance are open to the charge of medicalizing morality, but some current concepts of psychopathy and personality disorder are scientifically defensible, and denote problems which are properly of clinical concern. It is argued that personality disorders are mental disorders on the criterion of harmful dysfunction. Resistance to the acceptance of personality disorders as exculpating comes particularly from psychiatry, but this reflects a collusion with the law's archaic position on human agency. It is suggested that the social cognitive view of agency permits some rapprochement with legal views, but that the constraints on freedom need to be recognized. Personality disorder is one such constraint.

Whether psychopaths should be regarded as "mad" or "bad" by the criminal justice system is a topic already covered by a literature occupying yards, if not miles, of library space. It has also been debated at length by several Royal Commissions, the Butler Committee (Home Office/Department of Health and Social Security, 1975), and most recently the Reed Committee (Department of Health/Home Office, 1993). It is therefore doubtful whether there is much new to be said on the subject. Nevertheless, in this paper I shall try to identify some implications of current notions of psychopathy and personality disorder for this old question.

The question itself is, of course, nonsensical because mad is not the opposite of bad. Questions about badness or wickedness belong in the domain of moral discourse. Questions about madness belong in the domain of science. If it were that simple, we should have dispensed with the question long ago, but it continues to defy logical resolution because at stake are issues of professional power and ideology and the relation of science to morality. More formally, the question is essentially: should the presence of a personality disorder influence the legal disposal of an offender? This is a veritable Pandora's box. Not only does it raise the question of whether psychopathy is a mental disorder, it also invites philosophical arguments about why the law recognizes any mental disorder. I shall attempt an answer to the first of these, and touch on the second. First, I will say something about my understanding of the terms "psychopathy" and "personality disorder".

Concepts of psychopathic personality and personality disorder

A few years ago, I published a paper which asserted that the concept of the psychopath is "a moral judgement masquerading as a clinical diagnosis" (Blackburn, 1988). This was not, of course, the first time that psychopathy has been charged with representing the medicalization of morality, and on the face of it, this claim sides with the view that psychopaths are not mad. However, my argument was directed particularly at the concept of psychopathic disorder in the English Mental Health Act and the antisocial personality disorder (APD) category of DSM-III-R (American Psychiatric Association, 1987). It is therefore important to establish what might be a defensible use of the term "psychopath".

The controversy surrounding the term has reflected not only different meanings over time and in different clinical traditions, but also a confounding of the concept of personality with deviant social behaviour. Graham Foulds (1971) noted some years ago that personality traits need to be distinguished from the symptoms of illness. This is also recognized in DSM-III-R, which differentiates clinical syndromes from personality disorders. The latter relate to personality traits, which are defined as "enduring patterns of perceiving, relating to, and thinking about the environment and oneself". Traits constitute personality disorders when they are "inflexible and maladaptive" and cause impaired social functioning or subjective distress. Elaborating on this distinction, I have argued that social deviance is a further conceptual domain distinct from the universes of mental illness and personality disorder. Criminal acts or socially objectionable behaviours belong in the domain of cultural and moral norms, and are neither traits nor symptoms. Since these domains are not mutually exclusive, a person may be both socially deviant and personality disordered, or may be either or neither. Antisocial behaviour is therefore neither necessary nor sufficient to define a disorder of personality. The DSM-III concept of APD falls short in this respect because its criteria are predominantly socially deviant behaviours.

The English Mental Health Act category of psychopathic disorder is open to similar criticisms. The "disorder or disability of mind" it refers to lacks any referent other than its persistence and its power to cause seriously antisocial conduct, and in the absence of independent criteria the disorder must be inferred in circular fashion from the socially deviant behaviour it supposedly causes. It is therefore a legal fiction. It is consequently misleading to describe people who "suffer from" this disorder as "psychopaths". Not only is the label pejorative, it spuriously implies a homogeneous group who have something in common beyond their antisocial behaviour.

In fact, as the Butler Committee observed, "The class of persons to whom the term 'psychopathic disorder' relates is not a single category identifiable by any medical, biological, or psychological criteria". My own research with special hospital patients confirms this in showing that legal psychopaths are heterogeneous, and represent four distinct groups of deviant personality, described as primary psychopath, secondary psychopath, controlled and inhibited (Blackburn, 1975; 1986). Coid (1992) has also demonstrated the heterogeneity of those who receive the legal label. Using a structured interview to assess DSM-III personality disorders, he found that most patients in the psychopathic disorder category qualified for multiple diagnoses, the most frequent categories identified being borderline, narcissistic, antisocial and paranoid. There is, then, no single category of personality deviation exclusively associated with antisocial behaviour which would justify the notion of a psychopathic disorder, and offenders who are labelled in this way manifest a wide variety of inflexible and maladaptive traits.

There are, however, two further, though contrasting conceptions of psychopathy which have been influential. In German psychiatry, "psychopathic" has had the etymologically correct meaning of psychologically damaged, and for Schneider (1923), psychopathic personalities were a miscellaneous group defined by personality deviations which caused suffering to themselves or others. He excluded antisocial behaviour as a criterion of abnormal personality. The legacy of this concept is the broad class of personality disorders in ICD-10 (World Health Organization, 1992) and DSM-III-R. Cleckley (1976), however, rejected detailed classifications of personality disorder, seeing most categories as variants of neurotic or psychotic disorders. He therefore failed to distinguish traits from symptoms. He proposed a "distinct clinical entity" of psychopathic personality defined by traits and deviant characteristics such as superficial charm, unreliability, lack of remorse, egocentricity and interpersonal unresponsiveness. This specific conception owes more than a little to the psychoanalytic notion of an individual who lacks conscience or superego, and is sometimes referred to as the "classical" concept of psychopathy. This concept has been favoured in psychological research, notably by Hare (1986), and resulted in the development of the Psychopathy Checklist (PCL-R: Hare, 1991).

The PCL-R has sound psychometric properties and operationalizes a construct whose validity has some support. However, from a clinical standpoint, focus on the classical concept of psychopathic personality has two disadvantages. The first is that its relation to the classification of personality disorders more generally remains unclear. It correlates quite highly with the category of APD in DSM-III, but some of the criteria emphasized by Cleckley appear in other categories of the DSM-III personality disorders, such as histrionic, narcissistic and borderline. I have argued that this may be less problematic if personality disorders are classified in dimensional terms, rather than as discrete categories, with psychopathy representing one superordinate dimension (Blackburn, 1988; 1993a).

A second disadvantage is that only a minority of antisocial populations identified legally as psychopathic meets these criteria for psychopathic personality. For example, in my own research, only a quarter of legal psychopaths admitted to a special hospital showed characteristics approximating to the classical concept of the psychopath (Blackburn, 1975). Coid (1992) similarly found that only 23 per cent of male legal psychopaths and 31 per cent of females were "psychopaths" as defined by the PCL-R. This highlights the association of persistent antisocial behaviour with a variety of personality disorders. To restrict clinical attention to a more narrowly defined category of primary psychopath would deny many disordered offenders access to mental health services. I have therefore suggested that clinical attention is more appropriately focused on those offenders who exhibit some form of personality disorder, and not simply those who are psychopathic personalities in the narrower sense. I shall, then, emphasize personality disorders in general, and not simply psychopathic personality.

Is a disorder of personality a mental disorder?

Cleckley described the psychopath as having a "mask of sanity", but whether personality disorders qualify as mental disorders depends, of course, on what we mean by "mental disorder". DSM-III-R defines a mental disorder as "a clinically significant behavioral or psychological syndrome or pattern that occurs in a person and that is associated with present distress or disability or with a significantly increased risk of suffering death, pain, disability, or an important loss of freedom". Personality disorders clearly qualify as mental disorders by this definition since they are defined by disabling behavioural patterns. It is worth noting that there is no necessary implication of bodily disease in this definition, which takes the wind out of the sails of some critics of the medical model.

The DSM-III-R definition, however, focuses on effects rather than causes. There are still many psychiatrists who assume that most serious mental disorders are caused by bodily abnormalities. Indeed, one of the reasons why so many psychiatrists are unwilling to accept responsibility for personality disorders is that they do not sit comfortably with the traditional medical notion of a disease. However, the concept of disease has proved problematic in medicine. For example, the idea that illness always involves structural pathology excludes conditions without a known physical cause, which are therefore described more neutrally as disorders. Also, many illnesses do not have a single cause. There have therefore been several attempts to reformulate the disease concept. Kendell (1975), for example, proposed restricting the term to statistical abnormalities which confer "biological disadvantage" in terms of increased mortality and reduced fertility. On these criteria, the psychoses, some sexual deviations, drug dependence and possibly some neuroses and personality disorders qualify as diseases. However, this would disqualify some common conditions, such as tooth decay, from the realm of disease.

A more radical alternative was offered by Boorse (1975; 1976). He argues that disease is defined by functional rather than structural abnormality, and that the idea of a mental disease is a legitimate analogy. He proposes that the essence of disease is an interference in natural functioning, which applies equally to physical and mental processes. In this functional approach, what is unhealthy must be determined empirically, but relates to what contributes causally to goals pursued by individuals as part of their natural biological design (e.g. survival and reproduction). While accepting a materialist view of mind, Boorse argues that this does not imply a physical pathology of the brain. The defining property of mental disease is that mental events (beliefs, feelings, experiences) causally impair natural mental functioning. Mental illness, therefore, is not necessarily a consequence of bodily disease.

Boorse's view provides a defence of the mental illness analogy which avoids biological reductionism. It also seems a plausible defence against the claim made by Bean (1983) that psychiatry, and by the same token clinical psychology, are simply normative disciplines governed by social values, and are not applied sciences. However, in a recent analysis, Wakefield (1992) argues that concepts of disease or disorder necessarily entail values, since they are confined to conditions harmful to the person according to prevailing cultural standards. He proposes that what defines mental disorder is harmful dysfunction, i.e. conditions depriving a person of some socially valued benefit which result from the inability of some mental mechanism to perform its natural function.

Identifying the natural function of mental activities is a daunting task for theory and research, but the functional concept of mental abnormality as deviation from natural design provides a coherent framework for conceptualizing mental disorders. Richters and Cicchetti (1993) applied this concept in attempting to distinguish pathology in childhood conduct disorder from the effects of adverse environmental conditions. Conduct disorder has been found to be associated with a number of longer-term disadvantages, and there is evidence that a variety of underlying mechanisms central to the regulation of emotion, cognition, and behaviour play causal roles in the emergence and maintenance of this disorder. Richters and Cicchetti review evidence for neuropsychological deficits, psychobiological deficits, social cognitive distortions, and attachment disorders, and conclude that when evidence on the effects of adverse environments is also taken into account, there is support for the hypothesis that the harmful dysfunction concept holds for some forms of conduct disorder and some of those who exhibit it.

Conduct disorder is a required antecedent of antisocial personality disorder in DSM-III-R, but comparable findings from adults identified as having personality disorders are less comprehensive. There are, however, some parallel data. Hare et al. (1988), for example, found evidence for less specialized hemispheric lateralization of language functions in psychopaths, and suggest that the cerebral organization of language in psychopaths is marked by poorer integration of affective and other components linking cognition and behaviour. There have also been several findings of psychophysiological anomalies among legal psychopaths in special hospitals (e.g. Blackburn, 1979; Howard, 1984), and some of my recent findings suggest distorted social cognitions in primary and secondary psychopaths (Blackburn, 1993a). Using the harmful dysfunction framework, it seems likely that at least some forms of personality disorder would qualify as mental disorders.

One objection to the so-called medical model of mental disorder is that it locates the causes of disorder inside the person. This is also an issue raised by sociologists who argue that individualized interventions with offenders deflect attention away from the real criminogenic conditions in society. Norrie (1993) similarly argues that ideas of badness and madness both share a focus on the individual, but that mental disorders can only be understood as part of the social world. The harmful dysfunction notion appears to overcome this objection, because natural functions need to be understood in terms of their social consequences. I would also argue that unidirectional sociological determinism is as limiting as biological determinism. As social cognitive theory emphasizes (Bandura, 1986), human development must be seen in terms of reciprocal determinism.

Legal recognition of personality disorder as exculpatory

The argument I have been developing attempts to resolve some of the issues about personality disorders debated among the mental health professions. There is, I have suggested, a good case for considering those with personality disorders to be mentally disordered, and hence mad, as well as, perhaps, bad. What then prevents the law from acquiescing in this notion and from accepting that personality disorders may excuse legal blame?

At times, the law *has* done. Personality disorders have sometimes formed the basis for a successful plea of insanity or diminished responsibility, and for almost two decades during the 1950s and 1960s, American federal courts widely accepted psychiatric criteria of what constituted an exculpatory mental disorder under the Durham rule. However, there has been a swing back to the legalistic view that individual liberty must be protected by judicial constraint on non-legal experts, and the courts now tend to be conservative in their acceptance of mental disorder as a legal excuse.

Historically, the argument has centred on the insanity defence and the attempts to identify formulae that reconcile the law's concept of rational and freely choosing beings with the deterministic views of psychiatry. The McNaughtan rules required that for the insanity defence to succeed, it had to be proven that "at the time of the committing of the act, the party accused was labouring under such a defect of reason, from disease of the mind, as not to know the nature and quality of the act he was doing; or if he did know it, that he did not know he was doing what was wrong". The rules presume that everyone is sane and has a sufficient degree of reason to be held responsible for their crimes. They focus on the assumed cognitive effects of "disease of the mind", although this is actually a legal concept. As is well known, it is difficult for even grossly disordered individuals to meet these criteria.

Personality disorders are unlikely to form the basis for a successful insanity plea under this cognitive test, but the door was opened when the notion of loss of volitional control in the form of the irresistible impulse became accepted by the courts. This was always controversial because of the problem of distinguishing lack of resistance to a presumed impulse to act from mere unwillingness to resist. Nevertheless, in the United States, the two prongs of the cognitive and the volitional tests became a widely accepted alternative to McNaughtan during the 1960s. The test proposed by the American Law Institute (ALI), for example, states that "a person is not responsible for criminal conduct if at the time of such conduct as a result of mental disease or defect he lacks substantial capacity to appreciate the criminality of his conduct or to conform his conduct to the requirements of law".

The ALI test formed the basis for the defence of John Hinckley, who shot at President Reagan in 1982, and who received an insanity verdict on the basis of his personality disorder. As in the earlier case of McNaughtan, the verdict provoked a public demand for reform, and the idea that the bad were being let off punishment by being identified as mad was widely canvassed. As a result, the American Psychiatric Association (1983) hastily established its law and order credentials by adopting the Bonnie Rule. This proposes that a defendant should be found not guilty by reason of insanity if "as a result of mental disease or defect he was unable to appreciate the wrongfulness of his conduct at the time of the offence". This reverts to the cognitive test of McNaughtan. The Association argued that it was scientifically more feasible for psychiatrists to establish reliable judgements of cognitive than of volitional defects. It added that the "mental disease" recognized in the defence should be restricted to "serious" mental disorders of the severity of the psychoses, and should hence exclude personality disorders. The other APA (American Psychological Association, 1984) described this as hasty and not based on empirical evidence. However, the Bonnie Rule was adopted in federal courts in 1984.

An article by Rachlin et al. (1984) supporting the decision to exclude personality disorders from the insanity defence unashamedly reveals the motivation behind this move. They suggested that "the specific omission of the volitional component would go a long way toward elimination of the abuse of this defence and, in turn, reduction of public and professional outrage at getting away with murder". They later argue that "our proposals would send to psychiatric hospitals for treatment only those who belong there". These views provide strong ammunition for the argument that the insanity defence is more about ideological tensions between psychiatry and law than it is about technical matters (Norrie, 1993), and that psychiatry is prepared to collude with the legal concept of a free agent when it is in its professional interests.

In Britain, the insanity defence has become almost of academic interest following the 1957 Homicide Act and the 1959 Mental Health Act. Strange though it may seem, the provisions for diverting mentally disordered offenders to the mental health system are actually more liberal in Britain than in most other countries. They include the diversion of serious offenders with personality disorders. One reason, perhaps, is that since most of these have been found guilty, the legal view of the free agent has been affirmed, and little is lost by mitigating the sentence. However, concerns about letting off the bad by categorizing them legally as "psychopaths" have again arisen and were expressed in the 1983 revisions of the Mental Health Act. This imposed treatability criteria on hospital orders for psychopathic disorder. Many psychiatrists go further and argue that those deemed psychopathic on legal criteria should receive a finite prison sentence and be transferred to hospital only if there is a clear prospect of successful treatment.

Implications for psychological models

I have meandered through the medico-legal history to bring out two points about the barriers to accepting psychopaths as mad, which I believe have implications for psychological models. The first is that resistance to the acceptance of personality disorders as candidates for health care rather than legal punishment has come increasingly from within psychiatry itself. Whether or not this reflects self-interest, the argument mounted by psychiatrists has been that personality disorders are untreatable. However, evidence to support this contention is lacking. The voluminous literature on the treatment of "psychopaths" is for the most part concerned with vaguely defined samples exposed to poorly described programmes with uncertain goals. Where outcome has been evaluated, it has usually been in terms of reoffending. Two recent reviews agree that methodological deficiencies in this research preclude any clear conclusions about whether or not psychopaths are treatable (Blackburn, 1993b; Dolan and Coid, 1993).

From their study of Broadmoor, Dell and Robertson (1988) concluded that psychiatry lacks a medical model to guide the treatment of personality disorders. There are, however, psychological models of intervention developing in the cognitive and interpersonal fields (Kiesler, 1986; Beck and Freeman, 1990; Benjamin, 1993), and I believe that psychologists in Britain should be paying more attention to these psychological disorders. The therapeutic vacuum will be filled by other disciplines if we continue to neglect distinctions between criminal acts, dysfunctional traits of personality disorder, and symptoms of emotional disorder.

A second obstacle to accepting the position that psychopaths should be candidates for treatment rather than punishment is the ideological commitment of the law to the idea of the free individual. Apart from some psychotherapists, psychiatrists seem ambivalent about determinism, apparently taking the law's view that only in serious mental disorders is behaviour unfree. The BPS Working Party on the Butler Report (British Psychological Society, 1975) took a firmer line on determinism. At base, it argued, all of our behaviour is determined, and hence none of us can be strictly held accountable for criminal acts. However, I suggest that the idea may be dawning that freedom and determinism reflect a continuum rather than a dichotomy. Social cognitive theory, for example, has attempted to grasp the nettle of human agency, and in developing the idea of reciprocal determinism, Bandura (1989) has argued that we are all partial authors of our fate. The implication is that although there are always constraints on our behaviour, some of us have more options available to us than others. Personality disorder reduces these options.

The Butler Committee suggested that the weakness of the McNaughtan rules lay in "the now obsolete belief in the pre-eminent role of reason in controlling social behaviour". This would now be difficult to sustain in the face of "the cognitive revolution". However, the Committee equivocated on the role of reasoning by restricting its recommended alternative to the insanity defence ("not guilty on evidence of mental disorder") to severe mental illness or subnormality. This is very similar to the proposals of the APA nearly a decade later. The criteria proposed emphasize impaired reasoning, for example, delusional appraisal and misinterpretation, and thinking so disordered as to prevent reasonable appraisal of the patient's situation. These criteria are particularly strained by theoretical developments which point to the determining role of cognitive dysfunction in neurotic and personality disorders. And if personality disordered offenders are no more responsible for holding their irrational belief systems than are paranoid schizophrenic offenders for their delusions, why should they be held more culpable for acting on them?

References

AMERICAN PSYCHIATRIC ASSOCIATION (1983) American Psychiatric Association statement on the insanity defense. **American Journal of Psychiatry, 140,** 681-688

AMERICAN PSYCHIATRIC ASSOCIATION (1987) **Diagnostic and Statistical Manual of Mental Disorders** (third edition, revised). Washington DC: American Psychiatric Association

AMERICAN PSYCHOLOGICAL ASSOCIATION (1984) Text of position on insanity defense. **APA Monitor, 15,** 11

BANDURA, A. (1986) **Social Foundations Of Thought and Action.** Englewood Cliffs, NJ: Prentice-Hall

BANDURA, A. (1989). Human agency in social cognitive theory. **American Psychologist, 44,** 1175-1184

BEAN, P. (1983) The nature of psychiatric theory. In P. Bean (Ed.) **Mental Illness: Changes and trends.** Chichester: Wiley

BECK, A. T., and FREEMAN, A. (1990) **Cognitive Therapy of Personality Disorders.** New York: Guilford

BENJAMIN, L. S. (1993) **Interpersonal Diagnosis and Treatment of Personality Disorders.** New York: Guilford Press

BLACKBURN, R. (1975) An empirical classification of psychopathic personality. **British Journal of Psychiatry, 127,** 456-460

BLACKBURN, R. (1979) Cortical and autonomic arousal in primary and secondary psychopaths. **Psychophysiology, 16,** 143-150

BLACKBURN, R. (1986) Patterns of personality deviation among violent offenders: replication and extension of an empirical taxonomy. **British Journal of Criminology, 26,** 254-269

BLACKBURN, R. (1988) On moral judgements and personality disorders: the myth of the psychopathic personality revisited. **British Journal of Psychiatry, 153,** 505-512

BLACKBURN, R. (1993a). Psychopathy, personality disorder, and aggression: A cognitive-interpersonal analysis. In L. Klose (Ed.) **Proceedings of the Fourth Symposium on Violence and Aggression.** Saskatoon: University of Saskatchewan and Regional Psychiatric Centre

BLACKBURN, R. (1993b). Clinical programmes with psychopaths. In K. Howells and C. R. Hollin (Eds) **Clinical Approaches to the Mentally Disordered Offender.** Chichester: Wiley

BOORSE, C. (1975) On the distinction between disease and illness. **Philosophy and Public Affairs, 5,** 49-68

BOORSE, C. (1976) What a theory of mental health should be. **Journal for the Theory of Social Behaviour, 6,** 61-84

BRITISH PSYCHOLOGICAL SOCIETY (1973) Memorandum of evidence to the Butler Committee on the law relating to the mentally abnormal offender. **Bulletin of the British Psychological Society, 26,** 331-342

CLECKLEY, H. (1976) **The Mask of Sanity** (sixth edition). St Louis, MO: Mosby

COID, J. W. (1992) DSM-III diagnosis in criminal psychopaths: a way forward. **Criminal Behaviour and Mental Health, 2,** 78-94

DELL, S., and ROBERTSON, G. (1988) **Sentenced to Hospital: Offenders in Broadmoor** (Maudsley Monographs, 32). Oxford: Oxford University Press

DEPARTMENT OF HEALTH/HOME OFFICE (1993) **Report of the Working Group on Psychopathic Disorder.** London: HMSO

DOLAN, B., and COID, J. (1993) **Psychopathic and Antisocial Personality Disorders: Treatment and research issues.** London: Royal College of Psychiatrists

FOULDS, G. A. (1971) Personality deviance and personal symptomatology. **Psychological Medicine, 1,** 222-233

HARE, R. D. (1986) Twenty years of experience with the Cleckley psychopath. In W. H. Reid, D. Dorr, J. Walker and J. W. Bonner (Eds) **Unmasking the Psychopath: Antisocial personality and related syndromes.** New York: Norton

HARE, R. D. (1991) **Manual for the Hare Psychopathy Checklist-Revised.** Toronto: Multi-Health Systems

HARE, R. D., WILLIAMSON, S. E., and HARPUR, T. J. (1988) Psychopathy and language. In T. E. Moffitt and S. A. Mednick (Eds) **Biological Contributions to Crime Causation.** Dordrecht: Martinus Nijhoff

HOME OFFICE/DEPARTMENT OF HEALTH AND SOCIAL SECURITY (1975) **Report of the Committee on Abnormal Offenders.** London: HMSO

HOWARD, R. C. (1984) The clinical EEG and personality in mentally abnormal offenders. **Psychological Medicine, 14,** 569-580

KENDELL, R. E. (1975) **The Role of Diagnosis in Psychiatry.** Oxford: Blackwell

KIESLER, D. J. (1986) The 1982 interpersonal circle: an analysis of DSM-III personality disorders. In T. Millon and G. Klerman (Eds) **Contemporary Directions in Psychopathology: Towards DSM-IV.** New York: Guilford Press

NORRIE, A. (1993) **Crime, Reason and History: A critical introduction to criminal law.** London: Weidenfeld & Nicholson

RACHLIN, S., HALPERN, A. L., and PORTNOW, S. L. (1984) The volitional rule, personality disorders and the insanity defense. **Psychiatric Annals, 14,** 139-147

RICHTERS, J. E., and CICCHETTI, D. (1993) Mark Twain meets DSM-III-R: Conduct disorder, development, and the concept of harmful dysfunction. **Development and Psychopathology, 5,** 5-29

SCHNEIDER, K. (1923) **Psychopathic Personalities** (first English translation, 1959). London: Cassell

WAKEFIELD, J. C. (1992) The concept of mental disorder: on the boundary between biological facts and social values. **American Psychologist, 47,** 373-388

WORLD HEALTH ORGANIZATION (1992) **The ICD-10 Classification of Mental and Behavioural Disorders.** Geneva: WHO